Welcome...

"I enjoy all forms of photography, but nothing comes close to the passion and enthusiasm that I feel for portraiture. Whether it is photographing family or friends, shooting contemporary lifestyle images or capturing candids, I always enjoy the challenge of delivering high-quality, creative and appealing portraits. I've been lucky in my job to work with many of the UK's leading portrait photographers, who have provided me with a wealth of expert advice, techniques and skills that have improved my own photography. Many of these leading pros were involved in the tutorials and guides in this *Essential Guide to Portraits*, so you too will benefit from their mastery of portraiture. As you'll discover, taking great portraits doesn't demand you have the most expensive and extensive camera kit: a modest outfit made up of a camera and 50mm lens is all you need to take brilliant images. The more important factors are having a good eye for composition and detail, knowing the basic techniques of lighting, whether you're using daylight or flash, and above all, developing strong interpersonal skills with your subject. Don't underestimate this latter point – a relaxed, happy subject will always make for better portraits, so ensure you are confident, friendly and have fun while you're taking pictures. All the best!"

DANIEL LEZANO, EDITOR

Meet our portrait experts

All our portrait experts are regular contributors to *Digital SLR Photography* magazine. For further advice and inspiration to help you improve your photo skills, pick up the latest issue, available on the second Tuesday of every month. For more information, visit: www.digitalslrphoto.com

DANIEL LEZANO
An enthusiast photographer for over 25 years, Daniel specialises in portraiture and is author of several books, including *100 Ways to Take Better Portrait Photographs*.

BRETT HARKNESS
Brett is one of the UK's leading portrait and social photographers and runs regular photo workshops. For further details, visit: www.brettharkness.com

BJORN THOMASSEN
Bjorn is a successful portrait photographer, a master of lighting and leading speaker at seminars and courses. For more information, visit: www.bjornatinspire.com

PAUL WARD
Paul is a professional portrait and fashion photographer who specialises in location and studio shoots. For more details, visit: www.paulwardphotography.com

The Essential Guide to Portraits

Produced by *Digital SLR Photography* at:
6 Swan Court, Cygnet Park,
Peterborough, Cambs PE7 8GX
Phone: 01733 567401. Fax 01733 352650
Email: enquiries@digitalslrphoto.com
Online: www.digitalslrphoto.com

Editorial
To contact editorial phone: 01733 567401
Editor **Daniel Lezano**
daniel_lezano@dennis.co.uk
Art Editor **Luke Marsh**
luke_marsh@dennis.co.uk
Features Editor **Caroline Wilkinson**
caroline_wilkinson@dennis.co.uk
Features Writer **Jordan Butters**
jordan_butters@dennis.co.uk
Designer **Luke Medler**
luke_medler@dennis.co.uk
Editorial Co-ordinator **Jo Lezano**
jo_lezano@dennis.co.uk
Editorial contributors:
Brett Harkness, Ross Hoddinott, Paul Stefan,
Bjorn Thomassen and Paul Ward

Advertising & Production
Display & Classified Sales: 020 7907 6651
Advertising Sales **Guy Scott-Wilson**
guy_scott-wilson@dennis.co.uk
Sales Executive **Joshua Rouse**
joshua_rouse@dennis.co.uk
Production Controller **Daniel Stark**
daniel_stark@dennis.co.uk
Digital Production Manager **Nicky Baker**
nicky_baker@dennis.co.uk

Management
MAGBOOK PUBLISHER **DHARMESH MISTRY**
OPERATIONS DIRECTOR **ROBIN RYAN**
MD OF ADVERTISING **JULIAN LLOYD-EVANS**
NEWSTRADE DIRECTOR **DAVID BARKER**
COMMERCIAL & RETAIL DIRECTOR **MARTIN BELSON**
PUBLISHING DIRECTOR **JOHN GAREWAL**
CHIEF OPERATING OFFICER **BRETT REYNOLDS**
GROUP FINANCE DIRECTOR **IAN LEGGETT**
CHIEF EXECUTIVE **JAMES TYE**
CHAIRMAN **FELIX DENNIS**

recycle When you've finished enjoying this magazine please recycle

CONTENTS

TURN TO PAGE 134 TO FIND OUT ABOUT OUR FANTASTIC SUBSCRIPTION OFFERS

Setting up your camera

Your digital camera has a bewildering array of features and while this is great in some respects, the choices can be confusing. Here we explain the tools that you need to know when photographing portraits

Exposure mode Don't think about using the Portrait program mode – you're more than a happy snapper if you're reading this guide. Instead, select aperture-priority AE mode (A or Av), which lets you choose the aperture, while automatically setting the appropriate shutter speed. For most types of portraiture, you'll want to use a wide aperture to throw the background out of focus. To start off, use f/5.6, as this gives enough depth-of-field to keep the entire face (eyes, nose and ears) in focus. By selecting aperture-priority, you'll be using ambient light only. While flash has its uses, controlling daylight will give you more natural results and help you learn to manipulate available light.

ISO rating & the reciprocal rule In terms of quality, the lower the ISO the better, so start by setting ISO 100 or 200. Hand-holding your camera will allow you more freedom to move and shoot candids, but watch out for camera shake. The simplest way to do this is to use the reciprocal rule. All this means is you shouldn't let your shutter speed drop below the reciprocal of the lens you're using. For example, if you're using the lens at 100mm then ensure the shutter speed is above 1/100sec to reduce the risk of shake. If you're using the lens at 200mm then make sure the shutter speed is above 1/200sec, etc. Increasing the ISO rating is an easy way to achieve a faster shutter speed to avoid shake. Try not to go above ISO 800 as otherwise you'll notice increased noise in the image. In low light, whenever possible, we'd recommend you use a tripod. It allows you to use a lower ISO rating as shutter speeds aren't such a concern.

White Balance You should set the White Balance to match the lighting conditions you're shooting in. If you're working in mixed light and are a little unsure, then Auto (AWB) is the best compromise. Of course, if you're shooting Raw, you can always change the White Balance when you open the image on your computer. Something to bear in mind is that setting the wrong WB preset can be used to purposely shift the colour balance. For instance, setting Cloudy in daylight will add warmth to the tones, while selecting Tungsten will result in a very cool, blue cast – so be creative.

Image quality We would recommend you shoot Raw, as it allows you to play with settings, particularly White Balance later. If your camera has a facility to shoot Raw + JPEG, use it with JPEG set to Small/Basic. Then when you're reviewing images, you can go through the small JPEGs quickly, choose your favourites and work on the appropriate Raw files. If you're confident in your ability, and don't expect to need to make tweaks to the exposure or White Balance in post-production, opt for the best quality JPEG for optimum results and to save room on your memory card.

Autofocus With the vast majority of portraits, it's important that the subject's eyes are in focus as, more often than not, they're the focal point. Your camera most likely has multi-point AF, which allows you to choose between leaving all the AF points active or to select individual AF points. You could leave all the AF points active to ensure you don't miss a great shot, but you run the risk of missing the eyes and focusing on the nose as it's the nearest object to the camera. A better option is to select a single AF point and use this to focus on the eye. The central AF sensor is usually the most sensitive, so you can use this to lock the AF by placing the point over one of the subject's eyes, then pressing the shutter button halfway down. Once the AF is locked, recompose and fire. It sounds tricky, but with practice it becomes second nature. Another option is to select the AF point that sits over the subject's eye, this means you don't have to recompose allowing you to work quicker. If you intend to rattle off a sequence of shots with a very similar composition, this is the best option. If you do intend to lock focus, make sure your camera is set to single-shot AF as otherwise you won't be able to lock on your subject's eye.

Metering Your camera's multi-zone metering should be capable of exposing portraits perfectly in most situations. Take a test shot, check the screen and use the exposure compensation facility to add/subtract a little exposure if you feel the shot is too dark or light. Where your camera's multi-zone meter may falter is if your subject has very light or dark skin tones, is wearing light or dark clothing or is strongly backlit. In these situations, use exposure compensation or select the spot meter and use the AE-L (Auto-Exposure Lock) button to take a reading from a mid-tone in the scene, or from an 18% grey card that you place near the subject.

Setting up your digital SLR for portraits

A little unsure how to select the exposure, White Balance or AF on your DSLR? Let us show you the way via five popular cameras

CANON EOS 450D/500D/550D

(1) Set the top-plate dial to Av to select aperture-priority.
(2) Press the ISO button to set a rating. **(3)** Use the WB button to choose White Balance and the AF button to set One-Shot AF.
(4) Press MENU and select the metering option on the second tab: we recommend Evaluative.
(5) To set image quality, press MENU and select Quality in the first tab. EOS 550D and EOS 600D only: Press the Q button and use the four-way control buttons as a shortcut to all these key functions.

NIKON DSLRS

(1) Set the top-plate dial to A to select aperture-priority.
(2) Press the info (i) button and scroll to metering mode and select your choice with the four-way control. We'd suggest you start with Matrix. Press the info (i) button again and select AF Mode to AF-S.
(3) Set the ISO rating, White Balance and image quality using the same procedure.

OLYMPUS E-SERIES

(1) Set the top-plate dial to A to select aperture-priority. The other settings are made using the Fn button, four-way controller and the OK button.
(2) To set the autofocus, press OK, select AF, and set S-AF. For metering, press OK, go to the metering icon, select multi-zone and press OK. Set the ISO rating, White Balance and image quality using the same procedure.

PENTAX K-SERIES

(1) Set the top-plate dial to Av to select aperture-priority.
(2) Press the Fn button and press right on the four-way control to select an ISO, followed by OK to set.
(3) Press left to set the White Balance in the same way.
(4) To choose the AF mode, press MENU and the Rec. Mode tab, go down to AF mode, then right to set (we recommend AF-S). Set the metering mode in the same way (we recommend multi-zone).

SONY ALPHA: MOST MODELS

(1) Set the exposure dial on the top-plate to A for aperture-priority.
(2) Press MENU and select Image Quality (preferably Raw & JPEG).
(3) The following settings are selected using the Fn button and the four-way control. Press Fn, go to Metering and select Multi segment. Press Fn, go to AF mode and set AF-S. Press Fn, go to White Balance and choose a setting.
(4) Press the ISO button and set the ISO rating you wish to use.

Shoot & save
When you finish shooting, download your shots and archive every image onto a hard disk and a CD/DVD before you begin editing them. After editing, create a separate archive of edited images

OUR RECOMMENDED CAMERA SETTINGS FOR SHOOTING PORTRAITS
Exposure mode: Aperture-priority set to f/5.6 to begin with
Metering Pattern: Multi-zone
Autofocus: Use a single AF sensor with AF mode set to single-shot (AF-S)
White Balance: Match lighting conditions
Image Quality: Raw + JPEG
ISO rating: ISO 100 or 200

The basics of exposure

Our jargon-free guide about exposure provides everything you need to know to get to grips with apertures and shutter speeds

IF YOU'RE NEW TO DIGITAL SLR OR CSC photography, it's essential that you understand the fundamentals of exposure. Every exposure you take is made up of a combination of an aperture and shutter speed that determines how much light will reach the sensor. The aperture is the iris in the lens, much like the pupil of the eye, which can widen to allow more light through or contract to restrict the amount of light that enters the lens. Use a wide aperture and more light is able to pass through during a set time span than if you had selected a small aperture setting.

The shutter is a barrier in front of the sensor that moves out of the light's path when you press the shutter release, allowing light to reach the sensor and expose an image. The duration of the exposure is determined by the shutter speed. There is an obvious relationship between the aperture and the shutter speed in determining the correct exposure and this is selected by the exposure mode. While Full Auto mode provides point-and-shoot simplicity by automatically selecting a combination of aperture and shutter speed, and allows beginners to take great pictures with the minimum of fuss, the beauty and enjoyment of digital photography is to take control and directly determine how the final picture will look.

The first step is to take your camera off Full Auto and select one of the exposure modes that allow for far more creative photography. Follow our guide and experiment with apertures and shutter speeds – after all, it's not like you'll be wasting any film! Before you know it, you'll soon be creating imaginative images rather than just shooting snaps.

Exposure controls

Many beginners believe it's difficult to use aperture- or shutter-priority mode but in fact it's very easy to do. Once you've selected the exposure mode (1), it's simply a case of rotating the input dial (2) until the aperture or shutter speed you'd like to use appears on the top-plate (or rear) LCD panel (3). Depress the shutter button halfway and the camera works out the rest. It's as easy as that!

Understanding shutter speeds

Exposure settings are made by changing either the aperture or the shutter speed. The increments at which you change these settings are normally referred to as 'stops'. When you change a setting by a 'stop', you are either doubling or halving the exposure. So for instance, changing from 1/500sec to 1/250sec doubles the duration of the exposure. As well as full stops, you can also vary exposure in 1/2 or 1/3 stops depending on the camera model you use. The diagram below shows shutter speeds from one second to 1/4000sec.

Full stops	1sec	1/2sec	1/4sec	1/8sec	1/16sec	1/30sec	1/60sec	1/125sec	1/250sec	1/500sec	1/1000sec	1/2000sec	1/4000sec
Half stops	0.7sec	1/3sec	1/6sec	1/10sec	1/20sec	1/45sec	1/90sec	1/180sec	1/350sec	1/750sec	1/1500sec	1/3000sec	

Understanding aperture settings

The illustration below shows the iris at one-stop increments, i.e. each step from left to right halves the amount of light passing through the lens. The maximum aperture setting refers to the iris wide open (in this instance f/2.8) and the minimum aperture is the iris at its smallest setting (f/32 in this case). An explanation of where the f/number derives from would require an extensive scientific explanation, but the key to you understanding apertures is to learn how f/numbers correlate with the size of the aperture.

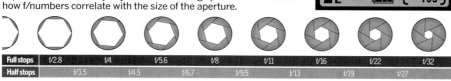

Full stops	f/2.8		f/4		f/5.6		f/8		f/11		f/16		f/22		f/32
Half stops		f/3.5		f/4.5		f/6.7		f/9.5		f/13		f/19		f/27	

Perfect exposure
Learning the basics of
exposure is key to ensuring
your portraits have the perfect
combination of shutter speed
and aperture.

Understanding your camera's metering system

Before you can influence the exposure, you need to understand how the camera's metering works. Here are some essentials that you need to know to pick the best metering mode for different shooting conditions

DIGITAL CAMERAS BOAST complex exposure systems and offer a choice of metering patterns, each working out the exposure in a way to suit various lighting conditions. A camera's exposure system works on the assumption that the area of the scene that is being metered is a mid-tone, or 18% grey to be exact; the average if all dark, lights and mid-tones were combined. It's a tried-and-tested method and the basis of all metering patterns. It's important to be aware of this when you're taking pictures as it helps you to know when you may have problems with exposure.

While this system is fine in the majority of shooting situations, it can lead to incorrect exposures when the scene or subject is considerably lighter or darker in tone than 18% grey. For example, very dark subjects or scenes can fool the metering system into thinking that the general scene is much darker than it really is and, as a result, will overexpose the image. Similarly, very light subjects or scenes can fool the camera into underexposing them – making them appear darker than they are – as the light meter will take a reading designed to render them as a mid-tone. It's in these trickier lighting situations, where the popular multi-zone pattern that provides the correct exposure for around 90% of shots struggles as it tries to meter the entire scene. It's in cases like this where using the other patterns such as partial and spot are useful as they offer more control.

As a camera is trying to render an image grey, it's your job to ensure you compensate to keep the tones true to life. To do this you have to overexpose the camera's reading to give a lighter result than the camera wants, or underexpose to give a darker result. With a portrait in a dark scene, for instance, the camera will overexpose bleaching the face, therefore you need to reduce the exposure. With a light scene, it's giving less exposure than you need, darkening the subject, so you have to add exposure to make it record correctly. If you're still unsure, don't worry, when you start shooting light or dark scenes and then try to override the camera's readings, you'll soon get to grips with it. By following our expert advice you should also increase the chances of keeping any exposure errors to a minimum.

Multi-zone metering

In theory, you could take every picture using multi-zone metering and never have a bad exposure. Well almost... The multi-zone pattern is the newest and most sophisticated type of metering pattern and the one most photographers stick to for the majority of their shots. While every manufacturer has their own type of multi-zone meter, each with varying numbers and shapes of zones, all work in much the same way. Basically, the entire image area is divided into a number of zones and when activated, individual meter readings are taken from each one of them. The camera's micro-processor then evaluates all these individual readings and uses complex algorithms to calculate the final exposure. To improve accuracy, many cameras also boast a library of tens of thousands of images taken in various lighting conditions, which are compared in a micro-second with the new scene to produce the exposure value. This system has proven highly reliable and gets the exposure correct more than 90% of the time. Its weak spots, however, are unusually light or very dark scenes or subjects. Multi-zone meters can also have trouble with very high-contrast scenes, in particular backlit subjects. This is why there are other metering patterns available, as well as a choice of exposure overrides, to help you ensure the perfect exposure.

Recognising the multi-zone pattern icon

Every camera brand has their own icons for metering patterns and below we show you what to look for on four popular brands

CANON

NIKON

OLYMPUS

PENTAX

How to choose metering patterns

Selecting a metering pattern is a straightforward procedure, but we've provided a guide on how to do it for a number of leading digital SLRs from the six most popular brands

CANON EOS DSLRS
EOS 500D users press the SET button, while for EOS 550D and EOS 600D users, press use the Q button and select the metering icon. For older models, like the EOS 1000D and EOS 450D, press the metering button on the four-way control.

CANON EOS 30D/40D/50D
Some older EOS models, such as the EOS 20D and 30D, have push button controls. With these models, (1) press the metering button and (2) rotate the dial until the top-plate LCD shows the relevant metering pattern.

SONY ALPHA MODELS
Press the Fn button (1) and select the Metering mode icon by pressing the AF button (2). Choose the pattern you'd like to use and press AF again to set.

NIKON DSLRS
For newer models like the D3100: Press the info (i) button and scroll to Metering and select your choice with the four-way control. Some older models like the D80 have a metering button you press to set your choice.

OLYMPUS E-SERIES
You can go through the MENU system but a quicker way is to press OK, highlight the metering icon using the four-way controller, press OK. Select the pattern with the dial or four-way controller and press OK to confirm.

PENTAX K-SERIES
Most Pentax DSLRs select the metering mode in the same way as the K100D. Press MENU to get to the Rec Mode display and use the four-way controller dial to go down to AE Metering, select the required pattern and press OK.

BJORN THOMASSEN

Metering options
Understanding how metering patterns work can help you when shooting in tricky lighting conditions, such as backlighting.

Centre-weighted average

Despite the arrival of newer patterns, this veteran still has its place on DSLRs and CSCs. This is the oldest metering pattern and was the number one choice until the multi-zone pattern was introduced. As its name suggests, it takes an average reading from the entire frame, with a slight emphasis given to the central area. While less sophisticated compared to the more recent patterns, its past popularity means it is still featured in most digital cameras, as many experienced photographers feel more comfortable using this pattern. It is a good option when used in combination with the AE-Lock exposure override, (which is covered in more detail later), but if given the choice, we'd recommend that you stick to multi-zone metering

Recognising the centre-weighted icon

You will find the centre-weighted pattern on your camera but you rarely need to use it in preference to multi-zone metering

Spot and partial metering

This is a great pattern when you want to take a reading from a specific area of the frame – but it must be used with care. While multi-zone metering takes measurements from the entire image area, spot and partial metering concentrates on the central area of the frame (you can see the measuring circle at the centre of the viewfinder screen). This allows you to precisely control where the exposure reading for the scene is taken from, as only the area of the frame within the measuring circle will be used to determine what's the 'correct' exposure.

Spot and partial metering is a great way to ensure that you get the proper exposure when you're shooting in difficult lighting conditions. Spot and partial are very similar in how they work. The main difference is spot offers a very precise measuring circle (usually around 3% of the image area), while partial usually measures the central 9% of the frame. The more precise spot meter is found on most cameras, while partial is less common, and a handful of cameras boast both. You must take great care when using spot or partial metering: always take a reading from a mid-tone, like grass or concrete, and not a light or dark subject, otherwise you will get an inaccurate reading.

Recognising the spot/partial icon

CANON (PARTIAL)

You need to select spot or partial by pressing the metering selector button and picking the respective icon. The spot icon is shown as a single dot at the centre of the rectangle, while partial is two small curved lines that form the outline of a circle. Some models offer both metering options.

NIKON

CANON (SPOT)

Remember: Position the spot/partial meter over a mid-tone to get the correct exposure. Spot-meter off a dark subject and you'll overexpose it and vice-versa. Try some practice shots to get used to how it works.

OLYMPUS

PENTAX

Exposure compensation

This is easiest and the most commonly used override and allows you to increase or decrease the exposure

ONCE YOU ARE AWARE of how metering systems work, and had a little experience using your camera, the times when the exposure system is likely to make mistakes become easier to recognise. The simplest way to override your camera's metered exposure is to use exposure compensation, which allows you to dial in a set exposure increment to increase (+) or decrease (–) the exposure. For instance, a subject that is significantly lighter than a mid-tone, like a bride's white wedding dress, is likely to be underexposed by your camera, so you need to select positive (+) compensation. If the subject is much darker than a mid-tone, for instance is wearing very dark clothing, then it is likely to be rendered overexposed, so you need to apply negative (–) compensation. Applying exposure compensation is quite straightforward and with experience you'll be able to judge how much is needed. All DSLRs have a dedicated exposure compensation button to make it a quick process in automatic or semi-automatic exposure modes. The compensation you set is often shown as + or – EV (Exposure Value) for instance, if you add a half-stop of exposure it will display as +1/2EV.

+1.5EV

-1.5EV

How does exposure compensation work?

Exposure compensation functions differently depending on the exposure mode that you are using. In aperture-priority, the compensation is applied by changing the shutter speed, but when using shutter-priority, it's the aperture that's adjusted. In program mode, the camera automatically decides between the aperture and/or shutter speed depending on the light levels so to minimise camera shake.

No compensation

+1 EV applied

Exposure compensation
This is a typical example of when a subject deceives a metering system. The camera attempted to record the scene as a mid-tone and as a result it's underexposed. Positive compensation of +1EV was applied to correct the exposure in the adjacent shot.

Exposure compensation
Set a + value to compensate for an underexposed scene, e.g if it's a light-toned subject.
Set a - value to reduce the exposure, e.g when shooting a darker than average scene.

Using exposure compensation

Your camera's exposure compensation facility is useful when you wish to make a picture brighter or darker than the exposure set by the camera. While exposure compensation is designed for corrective purposes, the effect can be used creatively. It's extremely easy to use: try applying '+' and '–' settings on subjects with different tones and see the effect it has. Here's how to do it:

1) Press and hold your camera's exposure compensation button (normally indicated by a +/- icon).
2) Rotate the input dial to select the amount of compensation. A negative value means you're decreasing the exposure, a positive value means you are increasing it.
3) The exposure compensation scale is displayed in the camera's viewfinder and/or control panel.
4) The compensation you apply will affect all subsequent shots unless you reset it to +/- 0 EV.

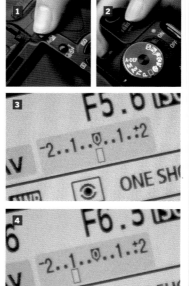

Auto Exposure Lock (AE-L)

Use this function to 'lock' your exposure independently from the focusing system to help avoid exposure error

AE-L PRACTICALLY EVERY DSLR AND CSC has an AE-L button, which is normally found on the top right of the camera's rear, or near the LCD monitor. AE-L is an abbreviation for Auto Exposure Lock. It is designed to secure the current exposure setting so that it doesn't change when you recompose your image, even if the incoming light levels change. AE-L can be used in any exposure mode, although it is pointless if you are shooting in manual.

When you press the shutter button down halfway, you engage the autofocus and the metering system to take a reading. This is ideal most of the time, but what about when you want to focus and meter from different subjects or parts of the scene? This is where AE-Lock comes in. This useful feature allows you to take an exposure reading independently of where you focus, which is ideal if your subject is very dark or light or positioned in a bright or dim area of the scene. AE-L is most commonly used with the spot or centre-weighted metering pattern to 'lock' the reading taken from a specific area of the frame. This is particularly useful in tricky lighting conditions that can fool your metering system, such as backlit objects or subjects with very dark or light backgrounds. For instance, if you are shooting a scene containing a bright light source in part of the frame, your camera's multi-zone meter could be fooled by into reading the scene as brighter than it actually is and will underexpose as a result.

To achieve the correct exposure, you want to take a meter reading that excludes the light region. This is possible by taking a spot/partial meter reading from the subject itself or an area of the scene that is a mid-tone and saving the result with the AE-Lock button, before recomposing the shot and taking the picture. Using the same principle, AE-L is useful when shooting subjects that are positioned off-centre. AE-Lock is also useful when you want to shoot a series of images using exactly the same exposure settings. For example, if you wish to stitch together several shots to create a panorama, it is important that the shooting parameters employed for each frame are consistent – using the AE-Lock button ensure constant exposures for each shot.

The AE-Lock button is an essential exposure aid when shooting subjects with very dark or light backgrounds that can easily fool your camera's multi-zone metering into over or underexposure. In this instance, the very dark backdrop fooled the camera into thinking the scene was darker than it actually was. As a result, it has set a shutter speed longer than was required and so the subject is overexposed. In order to achieve the correct exposure, a spot-meter reading was taken from a wall to the side of the stairs. This reading was then locked using the AE-Lock button. The picture was recomposed and the image taken. The result is perfectly exposed.

Using AE-Lock

The AE-L button, combined with spot or centre-weighted metering, is one of the most accurate ways to achieve the correct exposure settings for any given subject.

1) Select your camera's spot (or partial) meter.
2) Direct the camera so that the metering circle is positioned over the area you wish to meter from.
3) Activate AE-Lock by pressing the button. On some models you have to keep it depressed, so consult your user's manual. AE-L may display in the viewfinder to indicate the lock is activated.
4) Move the camera and recompose the image as you want. Your exposure settings will not change, even if the incoming light levels alter as a result of changing composition.
5) Finally, fully depress the shutter release button to take the shot.

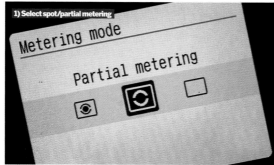
1) Select spot/partial metering

2) Position the measuring circle

3) Use AE-Lock

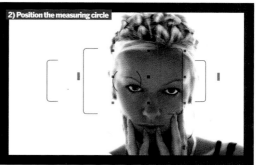
4) Recompose and shoot

Master your exposures for backlit subjects

Paul Stefan shows you to how to exposure a backlit portrait using the spot meter, a reflector and fill-in flash

Paul Stefan SHOOTING A BACKLIT subject (i.e. with the sun behind them) certainly comes with its challenges. Unless you know what you're doing, your results can be unpredictable and, more often than not, your subject looks flat and underexposed. This tutorial will help you to understand how to use the techniques you need to achieve great results.

It's easy to stick your camera on Full Auto mode and let it decide the exposure for you. And for portraits where the light shines on the subject's face, or off slightly to the side, Auto mode often works fine as the exposure levels aren't too extreme. However, if you position your subject so that the light source is behind them (so you're shooting towards them and the sun or light source), your camera is likely to get confused and the exposure terribly wrong. What tends to happen is that your subject gets underexposed, sometimes silhouetted. The reason for this is that the camera's multi-zone metering mode evaluates the overall scene. Given that you are pointing the camera towards the light source, it will always look to expose the shot for a bright scene, causing the darker areas – in this case the person – to be underexposed.

Taking more control over your camera will greatly improve the image and enable you to get the exposure you really want. One of the easiest ways to do this is to set your camera to aperture-priority mode and to use the spot meter along with AE-Lock to fix the light reading. With this method, you take a spot meter reading from the person's face, almost always resulting in a perfectly-exposed person. The only time that this technique may be tricky is when your subject is very dark-skinned. If that's the case, use the same technique but take a spot meter reading off a mid-tone in the same lighting conditions, this could be a piece of clothing, grass or ideally an 18% grey card.

While spot metering is quick and easy, it may cause your subject's surrounding scene to be overexposed if it's lighter than your subject. If you want to include the environment in the shot, one way around this is to take a meter reading from an in-between subject and then use your camera's flash to fill in the foreground with light, balancing the scene's overall exposure. Equally, a reflector can help as it bounces light back towards your subject for a similar fill-in effect. If you're feeling really adventurous, why not try a mixture, using both flash and a reflector.

✓ Try spot in manual
You can use the spot meter in manual mode. Change apertures and shutter speeds until the exposure scale reaches the correct setting. This saves you having to use the AE-Lock function

1 Take a shot with your camera set to Full Auto I was keen for my portrait to have a picturesque backdrop, so I chose a south-facing hillside near my home, with a view looking out to Robin Hood's Stride and Cratcliffe in the Peak District. My first shot was to see how the camera's Auto mode handled the exposure of my subject with the sun directly behind and above her. With this set up, I was shooting towards the sun, which would certainly challenge the camera's multi-zone metering system.

2 Using spot metering and a reflector The shot taken in Full Auto wasn't a disaster, but it could certainly be improved with spot metering. By switching my DSLR to aperture-priority and setting the metering mode to spot, I was able to meter from Emily's face and lock the reading using AE-Lock. I did this by looking through the viewfinder and placing the central circle over the her face then pressing the AE-Lock button to ensure a perfect exposure. I then focused on her face, recomposed and took the shot.

The result wasn't too bad as the face of my subject, my eldest daughter Emily, isn't completely underexposed, but it could be improved. This would have been much worse if the sun was lower and in direct view of the shot. Other DSLRs may not have coped as well as my Canon EOS 5D Mk II either.

Spot metering has improved the scene greatly, but to make it even better, I placed a portable reflector just out of shot, perched on a stick, to throw some warm sunlight back onto Emily's face. This made a big difference, revealing more detail and adding depth in her face and clothes.

3 Use fill-in flash

I like the natural look of the spot-metered and reflector shot, but you could make it more dramatic by using flash. I hooked up my flashgun to my camera with a sync lead so I could hold the flash unit away from the camera and over to one side. This is a useful technique that causes your flash to give a more flattering look to the subject, rather than blasting them directly in the face. With this set-up, I also left the reflector in place, used the same exposure settings from the previous shot and pointed the flashgun toward Emily's body, rather than her face.

The flash has made a big impact on how she's lit. Her face is brighter, but because I aimed the flashgun towards her body and feet, the shot has exposed her lower half so much better than the previous shot. Her hair is also really well exposed and she now has catchlights in her eyes from the flash.

240-4788

ISO100   0, 0, 0   sRGB

⬜-3⅓, 0, 0.   13/04/2009 16:08:41

Av ⬛⬛   RAW+⬛L 5.84MB

1/200   5.0   176/274

Portrait composition

There are no rules, only guidelines when it comes to composition but, like lighting, it has the potential to make or break a portrait. Developing your style takes time and practice but here are a few considerations to take into account and to help you along your way

1) Landscape or upright orientation?

It's natural to tilt the camera upright when you're shooting a portrait as it allows you to fill the frame with the subject's head and shoulders or entire body. It's a good format to adopt when you're trying to exclude as much of the background as possible to concentrate attention on the subject. Because this format is used so often when shooting people, the upright format is often termed the portrait format. Photographing portraits with the camera held normally to produce a landscape-orientated image often allows you to employ more creative compositions. For one, it means you can place the subject off-centre to include some of the backdrop in the frame. It also allows you to crop tightly into the face, which can add drama and impact to the image. Both options are worth trying while looking through the viewfinder to see which works best and, if in doubt, take a shot using both formats!

We have cropped the same image (see right) into a landscape and portrait format. Which do you prefer? The orientation you choose each time you compose a shot has the potential to strength or weaken your portrait.

Landscape

Portrait

2) Viewpoint

It's natural when taking a picture to shoot from your normal eye-level. However, while there is nothing wrong with this, shooting from your standard viewpoint is a little unimaginative. Also, it's not always the most flattering angle for your subject – you'll find that by shooting from slightly above and down on your subject, you'll capture a better and often more flattering picture. Experiment by shooting from a much higher or lower viewpoint to your subject and see how the results turn out.

Shooting a subject from halfway up some steps provides a very high viewpoint and produces an unusual and quirky result. Give it a try!

3) Breaking the rules: New angles to try

Use a wide-angle lens
Set your standard zoom to its widest focal length (or, better still, use an ultra wide-angle zoom) to photograph portraits with a difference. Because wide-angle lenses distort perspective, it's possible to create some very unusual images, where the part of the subject closest to the lens appears much larger than the parts of the body that are further away. It's not very flattering but definitely fun!

Eye contact
Yep, we harp on about making sure you get both eyes in focus with the subject looking at the camera, yet there are many stunning examples where the subject's looking away or their eyes are obscured. A lack of eye contact can add intrigue to your portrait or give it a candid feel, so don't be afraid of having your subject looking away from the camera.

Look how the wide-angle lens used on this shot has distorted perspective. You can get some quirky portraits from using unconventional techniques.

Shoot on a slant
Shooting images at an angle can add energy to an image as it displaces the balance of the scene. Give it a try, whether shooting with the camera in an upright or landscape format, and see how it can inject life into the image.

Frequently asked questions

Why should I not use my camera's Portrait mode?
While it takes the fuss out of taking a picture, scene modes like Portrait remove any opportunity of being creative. As with all scene modes, the Portrait program automatically activates certain picture-taking options. Depending on which camera you use, you'll find that setting Portrait mode results in the following: White Balance: Auto; Autofocus: Multi-point AF/One-shot mode; ISO Rating: Automatically selected; Metering pattern: Multi-zone; Built-in flash: Auto.

While these settings are suitable for those looking for point-and-shoot simplicity, for those of you wanting to develop your photographic skills, it's quite prohibitive and the fact that you can't control aspects such as the flash and White Balance can really affect the result you're trying to achieve. Instead, learn how to get the best from semi-automatic modes such as aperture-priority.

What should subjects wear?
The most important thing is that your subject feels comfortable. So don't get them to overdress or wear items that they don't like.

Ideally, ask to see a selection of clothing and talk through what they like the most and the types of portraits they want. You don't want colours, logos or patterns to dominate the image, so a plain neutral top is usually a good starting point, along with casual trousers or a pair of jeans. Tastes change so, if possible, opt for a timeless look that encourages them to love their portrait even longer.

How should I get them to pose?
It's vital that they appear natural and comfortable, whether they're sitting, standing or lying down. You'll find that subjects are normally unsure of what to do with their hands, resulting in them looking clumsy or awkward in the frame. A good starting point is to have them keep their hands in their trouser pockets if standing, hanging over their knees or between their legs if sat down. Buy fashion and lifestyle magazines and tear out pages where a model has a pose that you like, then show it to your subject and ask them to recreate it.

Have you got any make-up tips?
We asked professional make-up artist Fay Bacon for expert advice:
1) Always thoroughly cleanse, tone and moisturise the skin before applying make-up. It will help the products to sit better on the skin.
2) Apply an illuminator over the top of a moisturiser. This helps lift the skin and increase its radiance underneath the foundation, so skin appears more youthful.
3) Always apply foundation with a foundation brush as it reduces the amount of foundation used on the skin and prevents patchiness or lines on the face, making the skin appear extra-flawless and natural.
4) Use a translucent, loose powder and dust it lightly over the 'T-Zone' area. This reduces the appearance of shiny, oily skin.
5) Always use concealer for disguising dark circles and unwanted blemishes. There is an enormous difference between foundation and concealer; foundation evens out the skin tone while concealer covers. You need to use both for flawless-looking skin.
6) In terms of colour such as eye shadows, blushers and lipsticks etc, always consider the colour contrasts of skin tone, eyes and lips. Dependent upon the style and theme of the photography shoot certain make-up rules do not apply. However, most make-up artists would advise using lighter and more intense shades such as purples, blues and greens on darker skin and eyes, as this helps echo the beauty and vibrancy of the skin tone.

Pastel, neutral and darker shades are better suited for paler skin as they help intensify the eye area and the skin tone by allowing both to stand out more.

Put the 'rules' into practice

Consider your composition to capture fantastic portraits

Set-up

Paul Stefan TAKING PHOTOGRAPHS OF PEOPLE is something that nearly everyone with a camera does. Whether it be a friend, a family member or a professional model, it's often easy to snap away and end up with, well... a snapshot. A little bit of consideration for composition, however, goes a long way to improving your portraits. The standard 'rules' of composition remain the same for portraits as they do for most photographs. The rule-of-thirds, filling the frame and thinking about your setting/background are all factors that can drastically improve a portrait and determine its success. If used correctly and creatively, these guidelines will help convert your photographs from snapshots to pictures to be proud of. Read on to see the difference it can make...

1 Consider the surroundings

This first shot is an example of what not to do. Without considering the composition, you may end up with a nice snapshot, but the main focal point (the eyes) aren't in a third, making the composition look awkward. The building work in the background is distracting too and the green trees sticking out of the subject's head don't look good either. Thinking about the background is one of the easiest ways to improve your portraits quickly.

2 Left Keep it simple

As Rocky Horror fans would say: "It's just a jump to the left!" In this shot, the subject was asked to take one step to her left, this immediately improved composition by simplifying the background. Compared to the first image, you can immediately see the improvement it's made to the overall impact of the picture. The texture and tone is much simpler, keeping the viewer's eye focused on the model's face.

3 Above Getting closer

The placement of the eyes within the frame is paramount to improving composition. Generally, a portrait works best if the eyes are in the top third of the shot, as it guides the viewer from top to bottom. Getting a bit closer and using a 70mm focal length, as opposed to the 50mm used in the previous two shots, has meant the subject now fills the frame with more of the her face. Getting closer also helps blur the background more.

Final image

While the composition could still be improved, it's a lot better. Here the frame has been filled even more with a subject's face to create an intimate portrait. The focal points (eyes and hair band) have also been moved to the upper left third and shot at an angle for a more dynamic look. A wider aperture of f/6.3 has also completely blurred the background for a more pleasing result.

Breaking rules is child's play!

Now you've learnt the rules, it's about time you broke them

Paul Stefan APPLYING THE GUIDELINES of composition is a great way of improving your portrait photographs instantly. But, as you'll no doubt have discovered, sometimes rules are there to be broken, and when it comes to the composition, breaking these rules can lead to quirky results.

Instead of using a typical portrait lens like a 50mm, here I've opted to use a 17-40mm wide-angle zoom at its widest focal length. This type of lens can often be very unflattering for a portrait, as your model can end up with distorted features, so composition becomes even more important! You should still pay particular attention to elements such as the rule-of-thirds, your subject's background and so on, but don't be afraid to consider these more as guidelines than rules. You should look for unconventional ways of approaching a portrait, bending the rules a little to get a more unusual and creative portrait.

Set-up

1 Don't disregard all the rules

This first shot, using the zoom set at 17mm, gives a very distorted view of the subject and is a good example of how not to bend the rules. Little thought has been given to the position of the eyes, which is usually the focal point, so they have ended up in the centre of the frame. Nor has much attention been paid to what's going on in the background. The angle also makes the composition look a little too awkward, although the legs are working well as lead-in lines.

2 Left Play with perspective Shot at
17mm, this image is dramatic: the model has turned around to fill the frame and the lens provides awesome distortion. Although the model's eyes aren't on a third, having the lead-in line created by the elbow does means it works better than the previous shot.

3 Above Creative focusing Instead of
concentrating on the subject's eyes, the focus is on the leaves. Using f/4 has blurred her face, which is not something you would usually want to do with a portrait. It's made the image more intriguing and with a wider angle, I've been able to place the two main subjects at the top and the bottom of the image.

Final image

This shot combines all the best elements of the other images. Using the wide-angle lens, the model was shot from above with an aperture of f/4. The eye remains the focal point and the background has been simplified with a single texture, so it enhances rather than distracts. The quirky angle and unconventional crop works well with this shot too.

Take great portraits with no direct eye contact

It changes the connection between the viewer and subject, alters the mood of a portrait and gives you the chance to show your subject in a different way. So give it a go: break the rules and try avoiding eye contact

WHEN A SUBJECT LOOKS STRAIGHT at the camera, it creates an immediate connection between them and the viewer that's defined by the expression on the subject's face. Whether they seem happy, seductive or angry, all elicit very different reactions in the viewer. Focusing on the eyes and using direct eye contact has become one of the golden guidelines for good portraiture, as it grabs the attention of the viewer. However, if it's mood and mystery you really want to evoke, your images could become stronger if you choose to break this rule.

Photographs without eye contact can also look less posed, more natural. When someone makes eye contact, it's obvious they're aware of being photographed but when they look past the camera, it takes on the curiosity of a candid and makes the viewer feel as if they're gaining a glimpse into a private moment. The two adjacent photos are good examples of this. The photograph below right has a sense of the unknown as it leaves us wondering what's got her attention and what she's thinking about. While the top photo, with the girl looking into the camera, has none of this mystery. When the subject doesn't connect with the viewer, the viewer is no longer involved in the picture, but rather takes on the role of the observer. Another example would be two people looking at each other, as the camera would depict their relationship with each other, rather than the viewer.

As well as trying portraits without eye contact, why not combine it with some of the other rules we have suggested you break in this guide. It's unlikely that an image breaking all the rules will succeed, so for each broken rule, complement it with a powerful obeyed rule. We've shot our model in a landscape format, instead of portrait, but we've obeyed the rule-of-thirds. We've also skewed the camera to the left to create a more interesting shape – but we've used a telephoto lens to get a compressed and out-of-focus background. Try mixing and matching these rules to see what you can do.

Right: Only the faraway look in her eyes and the half-smile differentiate these two photographs. But, while both are equally as powerful, they elicit very different feelings and connections with the viewer.

Direct eye contact
The eye contact in this image creates an instant connection between the viewer and subject.

No eye contact
It's not eye contact that connects us to this image but its inquisitive nature and mystery.

Ideas for images without eye contact...

■ Sleeping babies
Capturing the peaceful yet fleeting moments of repose can create some cherishable images. Images like this wouldn't have the same appeal if the baby's eyes were open. Use soft window light and a wide aperture to preserve memories like this.

■ Reflections
Normally an image with no eye contact leaves you wondering what's caught the subject's attention. But, with the subject wearing sunglasses, you're able to reflect the rest of the scene in the shades and bring some context to the photograph.

■ A private moment
By becoming the observer, the viewer experiences a glimpse of the subject uninhibited by the camera. Imagine this shot but with the child looking at and reacting to the camera; it would have a totally different feel.

■ Facing away
One of the easiest and most powerful ways to take a picture with no eye contact is to have the subject turn their back to the camera, so, again, the viewer feels as if they're not observing but sharing in the subject's private moment.

Subtle seduction
The fact that the subject isn't looking at the camera gives this image a stronger sense of seduction than if she had looked straight at the camera.

Focusing fundamentals

While the autofocus systems of cameras are highly responsive, we can help to improve their accuracy

AUTOFOCUS IS ONE OF THOSE THINGS that all photographers take for granted at one time or another. Half-press the shutter release and it does its job quickly and quietly. While everything is working well, you don't really need to think about what's happening and why, but taking control of the autofocus (AF) can help you improve, especially when your camera struggles to interpret what you are trying to do. Understanding how this highly advanced technology works will ultimately help you to use it more effectively in your photography.

How autofocus systems work There are two main kinds of autofocus system used in modern cameras: contrast detection AF and phase detection AF. In DSLRs, the latter of these is used most of the time. Phase detection AF works by taking some of the light entering the camera through the lens, splitting it into two and directing it onto a pair of sensors. The point where it hits the sensor tells the camera if the image is in focus or not, and if not by how much it's out and in what direction. This means that the camera can find the correct focus very quickly. The downside of phase detection AF is that it needs contrast to work. Phase detection AF also requires a DSLR's mirror to be down, meaning it doesn't work well in LiveView mode. This is when we need contrast detection AF – the same system that is used in CSCs. It works by continuously monitoring the overall contrast in a scene while focusing, the idea being that an image has the most contrast when it's at its sharpest. It was initially a slower method, but in the last couple of years has developed to rival phase-detection.

Autofocus modes The most popular AF modes are Single-Shot AF (known as One-Shot on Canon EOS DSLRs) and Continuous autofocus mode. With Single-Shot AF, you press the shutter release halfway down to engage AF and lock focus at until you release the button. This mode also prevents the shutter firing unless the subject is in focus. Continuous autofocus mode, on the other hand, lets the shutter fire regardless of whether the scene is in focus or not, and carries on focusing even when your finger is half-pressing the shutter button. It's the mode best suited to shooting moving subjects, as we'll see shortly. It's worth mentioning good-old manual mode too. There are times when autofocus is simply not the best option, and focusing manually produces better results, such as with night photography, where low light confuses AF, and macro, where focusing is so critical that it is often best to focus manually.

Multi-point autofocus Early AF systems used a single sensor at the centre of the frame. Cameras now use multiple AF points grouped to occupy much of the frame area. As a result, AF systems can now handle off-centre subjects and objects that move in the frame, not just those in the centre. The most focusing points in a DSLR is currently 61 (Canon) but the average is 11. Shoot with all points activated and the camera will focus on what is closest to you – handy in most situations, but with portraits, can result in the lens focusing on the tip of the nose rather than the eyes. You usually have the option of reducing the number of active focus points, which increases focusing speed and allows you to focus on a precise point.

There are two distinct types focus point. Line-type sensors are the most common, but least sensitive. They work in one direction and look for detail that crosses them perpendicularly (left-to-right) to focus accurately. Cross-type sensors look for detail in both directions, and are faster and more sensitive. The central focus point is usually a cross-type sensor, though advanced DSLRs have a number of them clustered together.

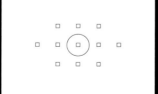

Single-point AF Select single-point AF and focus precisely on your chosen subject. Choosing the central point is usually best.

Multi-point AF Multi-point AF activates all the sensors and usually focuses on whatever is closest to you. It's ideal for tracking subjects such as a child running.

Setting autofocus modes on your DSLR

Selecting the autofocus mode and the number of active AF points differs from camera to camera. Here we show how it works on five popular models – you'll find your DSLR works in a similar way

CANON EOS (MOST MODELS)

AF mode: Press the AF button (located on the right side of the four-way control) and choose from One Shot, AI Focus or AI Servo mode.
AF points: Press the AF point selection button on the top right of the rear of the camera and use the input dial by the shutter release button to choose the AF point.

NIKON DSLRS

AF mode: Press the info (i) button and scroll to Focus mode. Use the four-way control and OK button to select AF-A, AF-S, AF-C or manual focus.
AF points: Press the info button and scroll down to the AF-area mode. Choose between Closest Subject, Dynamic Area where you can select a focus point for tracking or Single Point.

OLYMPUS E-SERIES

AF mode: Press OK and scroll to the AF mode option. Press OK again and choose between S-AF (single-shot AF), C-AF (continuous AF) and MF (manual focus).
AF points: Press OK and scroll to the AF Area option. You can then use the command dial to select all the AF points or select an individual point.

PENTAX K-SERIES

AF mode: Press the MENU button and use the four way control to select AF Mode. AF.S is the single-shot AF mode, while AF.C is continuous AF mode.
AF points: Press the MENU button and use the four-way control to go down to Select AF point. Choose from Auto, multi-point or spot AF (the camera uses the central AF point only).

SONY ALPHA SERIES

AF mode: Press Fn and choose the Autofocus mode option using the four way control. Choose between AF-S AF-A or AF-C mode.
AF points: Press the Fn button and then choose the AF area option using the four-way control. Choose between Wide (all points), Spot (centre point) and Local (manual selection of any AF point).

BRETT HARKNESS

Focus on off-centre subjects

When you are out shooting, it's not often that your subject will be slap-bang in the middle of the frame. In fact, we often go to great lengths when taking pictures to avoid placing the subject at the centre to ensure the image has the best possible composition.

If your camera has multiple focus points spread across a wide area then, chances are, these will manage off-centre subjects very well. For the ultimate control though, try selecting one individual AF point to take charge of exactly where your camera is focusing. The traditional way of handling off-centre subjects with a single focus point comprises three steps: using the central AF point to focus on the subject; locking the focus using your camera's AF-lock function; and recomposing the frame so that your subject is off-centre. Your camera's AF-lock is easy to use. Providing your camera is set to Single-Shot AF mode, a half-press of the shutter release will tell the camera to focus and then lock-in this distance for as long as the button is held down. It's an intuitive process, you'll soon find yourself performing the focus-lock-recompose routine without realising it.

By default, on the majority of cameras, pressing the shutter button halfway not only locks the focus, but also takes an exposure reading too. Try it yourself and see how your camera performs. You'll find you can usually use a custom function to set the shutter release to lock AF and the exposure together, or just the AF. Some models have a separate AF/AE-lock button, meaning it's possible to customise the AF so it's just the way you like it.

Use depth-of-field to give your portraits much more impact

By altering your shooting distance, considering your choice of aperture and focusing creatively, you'll stand a great chance at taking outstanding portraits

THERE ARE FEW, if any, more rewarding feelings in photography than capturing a portrait that not only pleases you, but has the subject over the moon with how they look in the shot. Most people have had their picture taken, but few get the chance to have their portrait shot. There is a subtle difference to the two: one is a quick snap, with little attention given to anything but basic composition and the other is far more creative and carefully considered.

It's often said that a good portrait captures a little bit of the person's personality and it's true. But what it also does is record the sitter in a different way to other pictures taken of them. By using a couple of simple techniques based around depth-of-field and focusing, you can produce distinctive results, as you will discover shortly.

The general rule for portraits is that you should focus on the eyes and set a wide aperture of at least f/5.6 to throw the background out of focus, while keeping the face sharp. The 'f/5.6 rule' is one that is used frequently by many professional lifestyle photographers, who like to work fast and prefer to concentrate on their interaction with the subject rather than changing settings. If you want to include more of the environment, however, a smaller aperture (usually with a wider lens) is required to keep the background, as well as the subject, in focus.

While ambient light is quite often sufficient – and sometimes ideal – you should also consider using studioflash. As well as allowing you to control the direction of the light, you can also adjust the intensity to provide the exact amount of light that you need for any given aperture. Once you learn how to use it correctly, a one or two-light set-up can also offer scope for creative opportunities.

Portraits can look exceptionally flattering when there's a shallow area of sharpness. The easiest way to do this is to use a telezoom set to its maximum aperture with a relatively short shooting distance. The result is a tight crop of the face where, bar a small focused area, much of the frame is thrown out of focus. The result is a very 'soft' image that, with

some thought given to lighting, can look romantic if lit by diffused light, or more arty and striking if used with strong directional light. When using this technique, be sure to focus on the appropriate part of the face, usually an eye but sometimes the mouth, depending on where you want the viewer's gaze drawn to. It's certainly worth giving it a go with a friend or family member and seeing how you get on.

f/5.6 at 200mm

f/5.6 at 200mm

Shooting distance
Both shots were taken using the same lens and aperture, but depth-of-field was altered by changing the shooting distance. The shorter distance gives less depth-of-field, which blurs the window blinds.

Lens choice

You can use most lenses for portraits, from the tele-end of an 18-55mm kit lens to telezooms like a 55-200mm. Using a longer focal length provides a more flattering perspective than using a wide-angle and also produces a shallower depth-of-field, making it ideal for eye-grabbing portraits.

Portrait top tips

1) Shoot handheld It will enable you to move more freely and frame quicker. Better still, use a monopod. Using the maximum aperture provides the fastest possible shutter speed, but if it's still low, use the image stabiliser if your DSLR or lens has it and/or raise the ISO rating.
2) Check your distance At very wide apertures, you have to be careful not to move forward or backward after focusing as this will lead to an unsharp shot.
3) Eye contact Ensure that the subject's eyes are clean and make-up has been carefully applied. Try some shots with the subject looking into the lens and others with them looking away.
4) Use the shadows Pay attention to the lighting and to where the shadows fall, as they can add drama to an image.
5) Consider mono It's always worth converting your portraits to black & white and seeing how they compare to colour images. You may find them more striking.

Differential focusing

Another popular technique when using shallow depth-of-field is differential focusing. It's a simple one to master but the secret is knowing when to use it. The basic principle is to use a very wide aperture to emphasise a particular subject within the frame by having it in focus while the rest of the scene (background or foreground) is out of focus. It's particularly effective when there is a lot of depth in the scene and you're using a wide aperture that blurs elements in the frame to the point that it's still recognisable. Use it to pick out a particular person in a crowd or to produce a creative portrait with a story to tell.

Hide and seek: These images illustrate the effect differential focusing has on an image. The same exposure was used in both shots but the focus was changed to reveal different elements in the scene.

Focus on nearest person

Focus on furthest person

Creative use of depth-of-field
Depth-of-field is one of the most creative in-camera tools, so think how you can use it to add an extra dimension to your images.

Master the art of selective focusing

By taking control of your camera's point of focus, you can make an image more interesting. Here's how…

Caroline Wilkinson
PART OF THE beauty of digital SLRs and CSCs is arguably the ability to control depth-of-field and determine what areas of a scene you want to appear in focus. You do this by adjusting your camera's aperture (the wider the aperture, the shallower the depth-of-field) and by manually selecting your autofocus point. Unless you take control of the AF system and select an individual point, the camera will automatically use whichever AF point(s) it decides is best, normally to focus on the subject closest to you. By being selective about what you focus on and how much depth-of-field you use, you can greatly improve your images, especially if it's a busy scene and you want to isolate a point of interest. It's a useful, aesthetically pleasing technique when done right, but very unforgiving if done wrong. If you use a wide aperture and your focusing isn't pin-point, the result can look awful.

Selective focus can be used almost anywhere and on anything to highlight the area of interest in your image, by blurring the rest of the surroundings. For portraits, you could use this technique to focus on the eyes, but that's rather conventional. Instead, add meaning, context and creativity to your portrait by making something else the point of interest, and the person a secondary feature. Both elements have to work together for it to become a quality portrait, so you need to find the correct aperture that doesn't blur the background (i.e. the person) out of recognition, but enough depth-of-field to isolate the focal point from the background. It's a tricky balance.

The point of interest doesn't have to be the closest thing to the camera either, but, on this occasion, it suited our image. Hands are very telling, especially those of an elderly person, and can be very photogenic subjects, with great detail and tonal range in the wrinkles and lines. Rarely are they made the focal point of an image, though. Here you can see that, by focusing on the hands with a wide aperture, using a standard 50mm lens and getting close to the subject, it's made them the feature and the person secondary. It's a far more creative and interesting image than if a small aperture was used to give front-to-back sharpness.

Camera settings

(Av) **Exposure:** Set your camera to aperture-priority mode so that you can concentrate on finding the right aperture for the scene, letting the camera take care of the shutter speed. If you're handholding the camera, however, be careful that the shutter speed doesn't get too slow, causing camera shake. If this happens, increase the ISO rating and, if possible, place the camera on a tripod for extra stability.

□ AF-S **Focusing:** Set your camera to single-point AF and One-Shot (AF-S/S-AF) mode so that when you partly depress the shutter release, the lens locks focus and remains locked on the subject until you release the shutter. As long as your subject stays still and you don't move forward or backwards, you'll get a sharp result. As default, the centre focus point is usually activated. It's up to you use it, focus lock and recompose (see panel) or select a point that's over the area of the frame you aim to keep sharp.

Focusing techniques

If your point of focus is off-centre, there are two ways you can handle it. As the central focusing point is the most sensitive, some photographers prefer to place it over the subject, lock focus and then recompose. However, if you or your subject move slightly, they'll be rendered out of focus, unless you repeat the process. The alternative is to manually select the autofocus point that covers the point of interest in the scene. With this technique, you can concentrate on the aperture selection as you won't need to recompose the frame once you've set the AF point over the area of the subject you want sharp. Whichever method you use, ensure your camera's set to single-point AF and One-Shot mode.

Here, the subject was placed by a window to create soft contrast with side-lighting. If it's too bright, a net curtain will diffuse the sunlight, or use a reflector on the other side of your subject to fill in the shadows. Set your camera to its widest aperture and stop down until you find the right balance for adequate depth-of-field.

X **Depth-of-field:** This is an average snapshot: taken at f/6.3 there's good depth-of-field making it unclear what is meant to be the focal point. Putting more thought in to the composition can also help emphasise the real focal point – in this case the hands.

X **Focusing:** By opening the aperture to f/2.8 and distancing the book from the subject, depth-of-field is shallower but it means the plane of focus is much thinner too. Here the focus point is on the book, resulting in the hands appearing unsharp.

X **Subject distance:** A change of viewpoint makes the picture more interesting but at f/5.6 there's still too much depth-of-field. As well as altering the aperture, you can also reduce depth-of-field by putting more distance between the subject and the background.

X **Background clutter:** Before you press the shutter, remember to check the background for anything that can distract the eye from the subject. Adjust the viewpoint to exclude any unwanted elements in the frame, in this case the picture on the wall.

Final image

To finish this image (shot at f/1.4), a High Pass filter was applied to bring out detail in the lady's hands. First, duplicate the image and go to *Filter>High Pass*, setting 5 pixels, and then change the layer's *Blend Mode* to *Soft Light*. Follow this with a simple black & white conversion (*Layer>New Adjustment Layer>Black & White*).

I AM THE BEAUTY OF LIFE

I AM THE NIKON D5100. I am new perspectives. With a large, high resolution vari-angle monitor, full HD movie shooting, 16.2 MP CMOS sensor, EXPEED 2 image processor, up to 6400 ISO for detailed pictures in low light conditions, and new special effects mode. I am full of creativity. **www.nikon.co.uk**

2 YEAR WARRANTY

For 2 year warranty on any camera and lens kit simply register your new Nikon within 30 days of purchase. Offer applies to UK & Republic of Ireland stock only. Call 0800 408 5060 or visit www.nikon.co.uk/register

At the heart of the image

Nikon

PORTRAIT LIGHTING

ESSENTIAL ADVICE & TECHNIQUES THAT HELPS YOU TO TAKE CONTROL OF LIGHTING

How to control daylight

Learning how to manipulate available light is an essential skill for the portrait photographer to master

WORKING WITH DAYLIGHT has several advantages and disadvantages for the portrait photographer compared to artificial light sources such as studioflash and flashguns. Daylight is incredibly versatile: the range of images that are possible, depending on the weather and the time of day, and the wide variety of lighting effects are tremendous. And, let's not forget it's free! However, unfortunately, available light has the problem of also being unavailable – both at night or on days of particularly poor weather when light levels are too low to justify the effort. One of the most wonderful things about working with daylight is that it allows you the chance to shoot outdoors in any location. Whether it's in the local park, a scrap yard or down by the coast, the options for great daylight portraits are limited only by your imagination and the ability you have to control daylight. And in the respect of the latter, despite the light source being millions of miles away, you still have plenty of control over how daylight falls on the subject, simply through the use of basic lighting aids such as reflectors and diffusers. Over the following pages we'll show you how using the most basic lighting accessories and techniques can transform your daylight portraits. As you'll discover, investing in a reflector or two and a diffuser – should you be really keen on shooting outdoor portraits – will really help to improve your portrait pictures.

Setting up your camera for daylight portraits

Exposure Before you head outdoors, take a minute to prepare your DSLR so once you're on location, you can begin shooting without delay. Firstly, you should set your camera to aperture-priority mode, as you'll want to ensure that depth-of-field is limited. We'd recommend you start by shooting at f/5.6. If shutter speeds are low enough to risk shake, raise the ISO rating to 400 and switch on image stabilisation if you have it.

Metering In terms of metering, you should find the multi-zone pattern to be perfectly adequate, but if you're shooting a dark-skinned person close-up, be prepared to add +1 to +2 stops exposure compensation.

Focusing We'd suggest you switch from multi-point AF to central-point focus as otherwise you risk focusing on the subject's brows or nose, rather than the eyes. Point the central AF point over the eye and half-depress the shutter button to lock focus, then recompose and shoot.

Also consider... While you can shoot with the White Balance set to Auto (AWB), you're better off setting it once you've arrived at the scene to the most suitable preset, especially if you're shooting in only JPEG. We'd strongly recommend you shoot in Raw + JPEG, though; this way you can review the smaller JPEG images on your computer. Then open and process your Raw files for ultimate quality, including any adjustments to White Balance or exposure that you need to make.

Which lens is best?

Using a telephoto focal length, which flattens perspective, is the best choice as it gives the most flattering portraits. You can get away with using the tele-end of your standard zoom, but you'll find a telephoto zoom, such as a 55-200mm, is a far better choice. Alternatively, you could go 'old-school' and shoot with a prime lens such as a 50mm f/1.8 (effectively an 80mm with APS-C sensors), which has the advantage of a wider maximum aperture than zooms.

Setting your camera for daylight portraits

Select aperture-priority, set the White Balance for the shooting conditions and centre-point AF. You're now ready to shoot!

CANON EOS 500D/550D/600D

1) Set the mode dial on the top-plate to Av to select aperture-priority mode.
2) Press the WB button and use the four-way control to select White Balance. Select the WB preset you want and then press the OK button.
3) Press the AF points button and select central-point AF.
4) Press the AF button and set AF mode to One Shot.

NIKON DSLRS

1) Set the mode dial on the right of the top-plate to A to select aperture-priority mode.
2) Press the i button and use the four-way control to select White Balance. Select the WB preset you want to use and then press the OK button.
3) Press i again and set the AF mode to AF-S and the AF-area mode to central-point only.

OLYMPUS E-SERIES

1) Set the mode dial on the right of the top-plate to A to select aperture-priority mode.
2) Press the OK button and use the four-way control to select White Balance. Select the WB preset you want to use and then press the OK button.
3) Press OK and set the AF mode to S-AF and the AF points to central-point only.

PENTAX K-SERIES

1) Set the mode dial on the top-plate to Av to select aperture-priority mode.
2) Press the OK button and use the four-way control to select White Balance. Select the WB preset you want to use and press the OK button.
3) Press the MENU button, then select the Rec. Mode tab and set the AF mode to AF-S and then select the central AF point.

SONY ALPHA SERIES

1) Set the mode dial on the left of the top-plate to A to select aperture-priority.
2) Press the Fn button and use the four-way control to select White Balance. Press the AF button and select the WB preset you want to use. Now press the Fn button again, select Autofocus mode and select Spot in AF area and AF-S in Autofocus mode.

The great outdoors
Shooting portraits with daylight is a great way to get to grips with the fundamental techniques of lighting and to learn how to use aids such as reflectors and diffusers.

Main lighting accessories for daylight portraits

Unlike when shooting with studioflash, when working with daylight you cannot control the light's direction or intensity. But while you can't control the sun itself, by using reflectors, diffusers or a combination of the two, you can control the amount of daylight reaching your subject. Reflectors and diffusers come in various forms, with the most common covered here.

Reflectors This simple accessory is incredibly effective at filling in shadows and can make a major improvement to your portraits. The standard type – and the one you should begin with – has a white side and a silver side (1). The white side reflects a clean, neutral light and is ideal when you can place it relatively close to the subject, as it reflects an even spread of light. The silver is far more efficient, producing a stronger result, so can be overpowering in bright sunlight or if placed too close to the subject, but is ideal in very overcast conditions or when shooting in shade. Gold reflectors are also available and, like silver, are very efficient, but add a warm golden glow to the light. Look for collapsible reflectors as they're light and easy to store. The larger the reflector, the wider the area they cover – look for a

minimum diameter of 80cm and don't go too big as they can be cumbersome. Those with grips, such as Lastolite's TriGrip, are great when you have no assistance, as you can hold it with one hand. Other reflectors to check out are those with a silver and gold slip-on sleeve (2) or with a lightweight frame, such as the California Sunbounce (3).

Controlling bright sunlight

A bright summer's day may seem the ideal time to shoot outdoor portraits, but only if you know how to diffuse harsh sunlight to produce flattering results

THERE ARE MANY BENEFITS to taking photos outdoors on a day when the sky is blue and the sun is beaming. Light levels are very high, so you've a full range of apertures and shutter speeds to choose from, even with the ISO rating set to a low sensitivity for maximum image quality. Also, because the weather is warmer, subjects are happier to sit and pose for you and you've a full choice of outfits for them to wear. Plus, because the light is so bright, colours tend to be punchier and saturation higher, which all help add extra impact to images.

However, there are also drawbacks to take into account. The first is the most obvious: sunlight is very bright and direct, so if your subject is facing it, they will most likely be squinting and their face and chin will have very harsh shadows, which amounts to a very unflattering portrait. Facing them away from the sun is one solution, but you'll then need to watch out for flare, as well as cope with a subject whose face is in deep shadow. The high contrast between the bright background and the subject also means that you'll have to be careful with metering, to ensure that the subject isn't underexposed.

The other solution, which we illustrate here, is to use a diffuser panel, placed between the sun and the subject, to bathe the model in a far more flattering light. In effect, you're shading the subject from the sun, but using a diffuser offers a number of differences to placing the subject within a shaded location. The nature of light passing through a diffuser is very non-directional, much like shade, but because the light has passed through a white material, it's neutral, clean and retains a relatively high level of illumination. Whereas in the shade, the light is reflected off surfaces, which, if coloured, will influence the light falling on the subject. And, because the light has bounced off one or more surfaces, it will be dimmer, meaning you have less choice with exposure settings.

The other key difference is that by diffusing direct sunlight, you're not limited in terms of location. You can shoot from the middle of a garden, beach or park, or anywhere else that suits your fancy, as you're able to use the diffuser panel to control the light falling on the subject. And as the diffused light is even, you can shoot from any direction, therefore being able to place the subject against a backdrop of your choice.

Shooting into light

If you don't have a diffuser, you can try shooting with the sun to your subject's back and to find a position where the sun is obscured from view. Using the leaves of a tree is one option, or, as in this example, a wide-brimmed hat provides a very photogenic solution. Use a white reflector to bounce light back towards the subject and either use AE-Lock to take a reading from their face, or add between +1 to +2 stops of exposure compensation.

Sunlit step-by-step

For this simple step-by-step, Daniel Lezano took some pictures in a garden using a Lastolite Skylite, which is a large diffuser panel that requires at least one person to hold it. Smaller panels that are easier to hand-hold are available, but bear in mind that the area of diffused light will therefore also be smaller. Take a look at the *Portrait Kit* section in this guide on page 126 for further details about the types of diffusers available. As you'll see, reflectors also have their part to play in manipulating the light so to better illuminate the subject and to help produce the effect that you want. In this shoot, the camera was set to aperture-priority mode at f/5.6 (ISO 100) and White Balance to Daylight.

1 Set-up Here's the basic set-up for the pictures. We're shooting around 3pm so the sun's still very high in the sky, and the diffuser has to be held over Ruby's head. You can see the large area of diffused light it produces beneath her.

2 Test shot This is the result of this basic set-up. Because the sun is obscured by the panel, Ruby isn't squinting and as the diffuser is just above her head, her hair has an attractive highlight. However, while the light on her face is fairly even, there are still some faint shadows that need removing.

3 Add a reflector To add a little colour to the diffused light, I place a Lastolite Sunfire reflector on the grass within the diffused shade, angled up towards Ruby's face. It's a powerful reflector, but as I'm positioned under the panel its effect doesn't cause Ruby to squint.

4 Spot-on lighting The resulting image is much better than the shot captured using the diffuser alone. The light from the Sunfire's surface has added warmth to Ruby's skin and has evened out the shadows. The result is more than satisfactory, but I'm not happy with the pose so I want to try something else.

Final image

I ask Ruby to lie down on her front and I do the same. As she's very close to the Sunfire reflector, the effect is too strong, so I turn it over to the white surface. Its effect is far softer and more neutral and, along with the pose, gives a better result.

Shooting in overcast conditions

Cloudy days are a blessing in disguise for portrait photographers.
We show you how simple it is to manipulate Mother Nature's softbox...

ANYONE WHO LIVES IN THE UK will know we're blessed with more cloudy days than clear skies and sunshine, even in the summer months. For most, this might not sound an ideal scenario, but for a portrait photographer it's perfect; a blanket of grey cloud acts as a natural diffuser, providing even, malleable light for you to control with ease using lighting aids such as reflectors. A cloudy day offers the greatest scope for manipulating sunlight as the angle, strength and tone of the light hitting your subject simply depends on what type of reflector you choose to use and how it's positioned. As there is no direct sunlight to contend with, you're also free to place your subject anywhere you please, even at high noon, without having to worry about harsh sunlight creating unsightly shadows and stark highlights. As you're dealing with flat lighting, to add a summer feel to your shots, try to have your subject dress in brightly coloured clothing and find an environment with lots of colour impact, like a lush green field, or head to a garden filled with summer flowers.

How well your subject is lit doesn't always depend on your environment, but often your skill in using lighting aids. As the light will be descending through the clouds, it is a good idea to position the reflector below and angled upwards towards the subject to fill in any shadows. Also try varying the distance of the reflector from the subject to get the light intensity you're after. If you're dealing with young children, why not have them sit on the reflector? It will fill in any shadows by bouncing the maximum amount of light back onto the subject from the sky and it doubles up as a 'magic carpet' – ideal for keeping those little ones occupied long enough to rattle off a couple of frames. Looking around your environment for reflective surfaces, such as marble or white-coloured walls, can also be useful for bouncing light onto your subject: watch out for colour surfaces, though, as they will reflect coloured light.

There are several types of reflectors to choose from, with a 5-in-1 kit being the best option for beginners, as they include a gold, white and silver side that vary in reflectance. In some scenarios, though, you may find the silver reflector is too harsh and cool, while the gold is too warm. In cases like this, you may want to invest in a mixed reflector such as Lastolite's TriGrip Sunfire/Silver reflector, which Brett Harkness uses here in the following step-by-step.

Create backlighting with flash

More often than not, bright sunshine won't make an appearance when you want it to. So, the next best thing is to use a flashgun. Mixing daylight with flash can, from a practical point of view, help fill in any shadows and, from a creative point of view, catapult your images to a new level of dynamism. It's a more advanced technique to tackle, but if you continue to practise it, you'll find it opens up a whole range of possibilities. One technique that you could try is placing a flashgun behind your subject to mimic a sunlit backlight. As your flash is off-camera, you'll need to be able to fire it wirelessly with a remote trigger. If you're trying this technique for the first time, set your camera to program mode and your flash to TTL. If you find that the flash effect is too low, boost its power by dialling in (positive) flash exposure compensation.

Handling overcast light

Working with kids is tough at the best of times, so shooting in overcast conditions is ideal because you can allow them to move around freely knowing you don't have to worry about harsh shadows or squinting in direct sunshine. We helped Brett Harkness on a typical lifestyle shoot as he worked his magic in very overcast lighting conditions.

Brett's model is a typical eight-year-old boy, unable to sit still for more than a few frames before running off to explore and play. The beauty of a cloudy sky means Brett can let him do this and then when the opportunity arises for a good shot, simply manoeuvre a reflector to improve the quality of light. When photographing your kids, or someone else's, remember to have fun: you're more likely to get better shots of them if you succumb to a few games than if you force them to comply with your shoot.

1 Set-up Having scouted the location for suitable backgrounds, Brett started by sitting his subject in front of a green door and set an aperture of f/5.6. As the light levels were low, we positioned a Lastolite Sunfire/Silver reflector to the side of him to create a little contrast from the flat, low light.

2 Test shot With his face in focus, Brett rattled off a few frames, encouraging the subject to give a few different expressions and to mess around with the grass. To get a more dynamic picture, Brett twists his camera to get a diagonal composition.

3 Alter position After letting the subject play for a while, Brett sat him on top of a mesh cage to stop him moving around. We held two Lastolite TriGrip reflectors below, and to the side of him, to bounce the light descending from the sky. We used one close to him and the other further away to create slight contrast in his face.

Final image
Brett's series of images captured a variety of expressions and poses. The reflectors worked a treat with the lighting and we used Levels to slightly boost contrast to give us this final result.

How to take portraits under cover

If you're ever struggling to work with harsh direct sunlight, one easy way to control the light is to step into some shade. We show you how to go about it...

WHEN THE SUN IS STRONG and high in the sky, there's often nowhere to escape its harsh rays and high-contrast conditions. So if you're after a wide, smooth tonal range with limited contrast and better control but you don't have a diffuser, your best chance for success is to find cover in a spot of shade, such as under a tree or beside a building.

Placing your subject in some shade instantly improves lighting and gives you more control over the strength and direction of the ambient light. Just remember that the light will be softer, cooler and more diffused, so you'll also have lower light levels to consider, as well as potential colour casts.

As shade is naturally cooler than sunlight, as well as setting your White Balance to Shade, you may want to opt for a reflector that adds warmth, such as a gold reflector or Lastolite's sunfire/silver reflector. You will also need to be aware of surrounding colours, because dark surfaces absorb light while pale ones reflect it. Watch out for strong coloured surfaces too as they may reflect coloured light, so don't place your subject too close and be aware that you may need to adjust your White Balance settings appropriately, or shoot in Raw so you can correct any colour cast later.

When shooting in shade, you need to be aware of where the light is coming from, which can be tricky as it's likely to be bouncing off different surfaces like walls and floors at various angles, but with practice you'll learn how to master it. By placing your subject in the shade, an easy way to control the strength and direction of light is to vary the subject's distance from the shade and sun; the closer they are to leaving the shaded area, the stronger the light. You can further control light by moving a reflector towards or away from the subject. You can also control the contrast by where you position your subject, for instance half in the light and half in the shadow or with their back to the light so they're backlit. If you try the latter technique, position a reflector in front of your subject to reflect light onto the face to fill in any shadows. You could also try turning your back to the sun, and have your model face you – it will cast a very flattering, soft and low-contrast light over their face.

Learning how to work with shade is useful when shooting on sunny days, especially if you're dealing with subjects who are wearing clothes that are near white or black in tone, or are dark-skinned, as in bright conditions it can be an exposure nightmare.

White Balance

Most beginners keep their White Balance set to Auto and normally get good results, but selecting the White Balance to match the lighting conditions will provide a more accurate result. For instance, by setting AWB, a photograph in shade looks very blue, but changing the WB to Shade will provide a warmer result. You can take things even further by using the Custom WB setting or one of the other presets to produce images that deliberately have a warmer or cooler tone.

Shooting in shade

We asked pro photographer Brett Harkness to show us his process for shooting in shade. This alleyway was perfect; it offered some shade and the contained light meant it was soft and easily controllable. To get the right level of light on Emma, his model, he had her walk very slowly from inside the alley, towards him and the light until he was happy with how her face was illuminated.

1 Try different settings As light levels were low, Brett started with a wide aperture of f/4 and cranked up his ISO to 640 to generate a fast enough shutter speed to shoot handheld. The first few shots he took were good but even though the background is blurred, there's still a lot going on. Brett zoomed his lens in closer to make a tighter head-and-shoulder crop. Much better!

2 Experiment with poses For a different shot, he positioned Emma leaning against a wall but by moving her the light on her face was reduced, so he brought in a reflector. We opted for the silver-strong side of the Lastolite Sunfire reflector as it gave the strongest reflectance and filled in a lot of the shadows.

If you're using a wide aperture you need to be very careful where you place your focus point. Here, Brett has focused on Emma's eyes using selective focusing, which has thrown the foreground and background out of focus. The wall also provides useful lead-in lines to Emma's face, strengthening the composition.

Final image
We picked our favourite and converted it to black & white. Note how the shaded light produces beautifully smooth skin tones.

Shooting late in the day

Daniel Lezano reveals the challenges and rewards of shooting in the final minutes of the day's light

Daniel Lezano THE 'MAGIC HOUR' IS A PHRASE commonly used by landscape photographers to describe the period of time early in the morning or late in the day, when the sun is so low in the sky that the light has a strong golden hue. For landscape images, this light can give scenes a three-dimensional feel as it creates shadows that reveal the depth and contours of the scenery. For portrait photography, this golden light adds warmth to a subject's skin tone and backdrop. You have to work fast, though, as you literally have minutes to take advantage of the setting sun before it disappears. You also need to be aware that you're at the mercy of the weather, as if it's cloudy, you will have little or no golden light to play with. However, if you are lucky enough to have this wonderful light appear, as well as shooting with the subject facing the light, it's also worth using the sunset as a colourful backdrop.

You're guaranteed soft light once the sun is low in the sky, as the entire scene will be in shade. This means you can work without any lighting aids, although even with low-light levels, you'll find reflectors still produce some illumination. The extra reflectance will come in useful when trying to avoid camera shake, as the very low-light results in a longer shutter speed.

To provide an example, I headed to a park to capture some shots of a friend's daughter. Ruby has blonde curly hair – perfect for backlighting. Rather than go for colourful clothing, I arranged for Ruby to wear neutral tones to complement the natural colours of the scenery.

With such a short time period to work in, arrive at your location ten minutes ahead of when you plan to shoot to spot potential viewpoints and backgrounds. I decided on the bank of a pond, as it meant the horizon was unobstructed and I'd have the light for longer than if I was to shoot within the park where trees block the falling sun.

I took a white, silver and gold reflector, which Ruby's mum was happy to hold in position. The white reflector, while a favourite for most daylight shoots, might be too inefficient to bounce enough daylight when light levels fell very low. In which case, the silver or gold reflector could prove more useful, although care would need to be taken with the gold reflector when combined with the already golden light from the low sun, that it didn't create too warm a cast.

As with the majority of my portrait shoots, I used my DSLR (with 50mm f/1.8 lens) set to aperture-priority, with the initial aperture setting at f/5.6. The White Balance was set to AWB and I shot in Raw + JPEG, to allow me to tweak WB if necessary in post-production.

Avoiding camera shake

Due to the relatively slow shutter speeds that occur when shooting at this time of day, avoiding camera shake should be at the forefront of your mind. The easiest way to do this is use image stabilisation if your camera or lens has it, stick to a wide aperture of around f/4-5.6 and set the ISO rating to at least 400. You should also use a moderate telephoto lens of between 50mm and 100mm, rather than a longer telephoto, which increases the risk of shake. Using the reciprocal rule can help you determine when you run the risk of shake. To do this, ensure your shutter speed is at least equal or faster than the reciprocal of the lens in use. For instance, if you are using a focal length of 100mm, ensure the shutter speed is at least 1/100sec, at 200mm use 1/200sec or faster, and so on.

With the sun's orb still visible in the sky, I position Ruby in front of a pond, with her back to the sun, to make the most of the golden colours of the backdrop. While the low sun creates a glow in her hair, the glare effect is too strong, reducing contrast and adversely affecting the image.

I move Ruby to stand in front of a tree and try shooting from a variety of viewpoints, remembering to alternate the format by taking portrait and landscape images. The texture of the tree adds interest and the golden light from the sun, to Ruby's left, adds a lovely warmth to her skin.

Before the sun has completely set, and the scene becomes totally shaded, the light still has a very slight touch of gold to it, adding colour to her hair. Positioning a white reflector to Ruby's left side allows me to bounce a little extra light in to fill any shadows, yet retain the skin's natural tones.

Going too gold!

Take care with the gold reflector: using it with a setting sun can overdo the warm effect, especially if the reflector is positioned too close to the subject. Save the gold for when the subject is in deep shade and try a silver or white reflector instead.

Final image of the day
By moving further away from Ruby, I can use some of the scenery to add visual interest to the image. By shooting in an upright format and placing Ruby off-centre, I used the line of trees to lead the eye through the scene towards her.

Add flare to outdoor portraits

Pro photographer Paul Ward shows how deliberately letting the sun encroach in the frame to add a touch of flare can work with portraits

Paul Ward NOTHING DIVIDES opinion like lens flare. Some photographers love it, while others abhor it, going to great lengths to avoid it. Lens flare is caused by direct light travelling through a lens and bouncing off its glass elements, usually having one of two effects: bleaching colours with a white haze, reducing contrast, and creating rings of colour (known as artefacts) that dart across the frame from the sun. Using a lens hood or shooting with your back to the sun helps avoid it, but lens manufacturers have developed such effective lens multi-coatings that it's difficult to create flare with some lenses. If you struggle, try an older uncoated lens: good quality secondhand manual focus lenses can be picked up for just a few quid. Artefacts vary depending on the type of lens, too: flare from a zoom will look very different from that of a prime lens, so experiment a little.

When using aperture-priority mode, you'll find that every time you change position, your exposure changes. You can avoid this by working in manual mode, but for the sake of beginners I'll show you how to achieve it in AV mode. Start with a test shot using between f/3.5- f/5.6 to get a shallow depth-of-field. The trick is to then position the model in front of the sun. Depending on how high the sun is, you might need to kneel and shoot from a lower than normal perspective. Winter, or early morning and evening are perfect, as the sun is never that high in the sky. Nearly every lens produces flare if it's aimed in the direction of the sun, but it takes the right kind of lens to give artefacts, which gives pro photographers that stylised finish they like.

Old lenses can create flare

Often older lenses create better flare because they lack anti-flare multi-coatings. If you're lucky enough to have only new kit that's not proving very effective, have a look on eBay for a lens adapter so you can buy an old lens to fit to your camera. I bought an 'M42 for Canon' adaptor and a 28mm Vivitar lens for £15 each. Car boot sales and secondhand stores are also good places to pick up a bargain lens.

1 Use a reflector As the subject is backlit, you can expect the multi-zone metering of your camera to produce an underexposed result. You could add positive exposure compensation, but there is another option. Using a reflector is an easy and effective way to bounce the sun's rays back on to the subject's face. A gold reflector gives a warmer light than a silver or white reflector, which suits this technique. If the model squints, have them close their eyes and then open them moments before you take the shot.

2 Focusing It can be tricky to autofocus on a subject when the sun is in the frame, as it causes a lack of contrast. To get around this, use the subject to block the sun and focus, keep the shutter button half-depressed to lock focus, and then move slightly to the side so the sun enters the frame. This can mess around with your exposure, so it takes a little trial and error. Depending on where you put the sun in the frame, it may cause too much flare, leading to blown-out highlights, so be patient and keep trying.

3 Exposure If the shots look too bright, dial in a couple of stops of negative exposure compensation or don't let as much sun encroach into the frame. If the shots are too dark, but the sun is as much in the frame as you want it to be, dial in a couple of stops of positive exposure compensation. For this image, as the sun is just peeping past her head, I used two stops of positive exposure compensation to overexpose, but it's slightly too much. For the next shots, I try to replicate the position of the sun and use one stop of positive exposure compensation.

4 Different optics The Canon EF 24-70mm f/2.8L USM lens I've been using is so efficient at blocking flare that I'm struggling to get any artefacts in the picture, and am only getting the haze. The more I overexpose the shot, the more streaks of white flare expand across the subject's face, which is not the effect I want. I switch to my new, 20-year-old 28mm Vivitar lens (not anti-flare coated) to see if it does a better job. With the model in the same position, I take another shot that produces some excellent artefacts running across the picture, giving me the stylised effect I'm looking for.

✓ **Position of the sun**
For flare to work, you need to shoot into the sun and have the orb visible in the frame, or at least just outside it, to get the whitewashed look. While cloudy days will produce softer light, shooting into the sun when it's blocked by cloud won't produce flare, but instead will only bleach the background

Final image
There's a beautiful balance to the flare in this image, it's got the lens artefacts and a subtle whitewash that gives it a stylised spring finish.

Have a ball with backlighting at the beach

Silhouettes are graphic and simple to achieve: read on to get expert advice on how to capture your own

Ross Hoddinott THERE'S NO BETTER PLACE to spend a warm, summer's evening than at the seaside. Maybe you like to surf, paddle or play – or simply relax by reading a book or topping up your tan. However, if you are heading to the beach with the family, whatever you do, don't forget your camera as there are endless photo opportunities to be had. Colourful skies are highly seductive and sunsets are particularly photogenic by the sea. With the sun so low in the sky, anything between you and the sun will be cast in silhouette. Personally, I love the simplicity of silhouetted subjects as they're rendered without colour or detail. Therefore, bold, easily recognisable shapes and outlines work best.

People are particularly photogenic silhouetted at sunset. The warm, evening light can create a romantic mood, so think about photographing a couple kissing with the sun setting behind. Children also make great subjects – holding hands with a parent, or just playing and having fun. You could try shooting candids on the beach, but ask permission first – particularly if photographing minors. However, you can apply far more control over the look of your results by photographing a family member or someone you know. Using a willing 'model' gives you the opportunity to experiment more, perfect your exposure and try again if your first attempts are unsuccessful.

With this in mind, I asked my sister if I could borrow my eight year-old nephew for the evening. She enthusiastically agreed and while she poured herself a glass of wine and relaxed for an hour or two, Tom and I headed to the local beach with the promise of a large ice cream if he would happily let me photograph him having fun…

Exposure compensation

TTL metering systems are highly sophisticated and reliable. However, that doesn't mean that they don't make mistakes. In awkward lighting conditions – for example, backlighting – they can easily be deceived. By regularly viewing the histogram, any exposure error is easy to spot, as there will be a spike of data at one end of the graph. Correcting under- or overexposure is easy using your camera's exposure compensation button. If your images are too light, dial in negative (–) compensation; this will make the image darker. If your images are too dark, dial in positive (+) compensation to lighten results. You do this by pressing the +/– (exposure compensation) button and rotating the command dial until you have set the desired level of compensation. However, the way you select compensation will vary from camera to camera. Most cameras allow you to set compensation at up to three or five stops in 1/3 or 1/2-stop increments. Note: it doesn't automatically reset itself to 0 when you switch the camera off. Therefore, remember to reset compensation after you have finished shooting. Fail to do so and you will apply the compensation to future images too.

1 Planning If you are visiting the beach to shoot silhouetted portraits, then plan carefully. Check the time of sunset, and its position, by visiting http://photoephemeris.com (or download the app The Photographer's Ephemeris). For safety, also check the time of high tide. Arrive an hour before sunset to give yourself time to set up before the best light and colour appears.

2 Set-up Use a standard zoom as it's very versatile. I use a Nikon 24-70mm as its fast maximum aperture of f/2.8 provides a bright viewfinder image, aiding focusing and composition – perfect for low-light photography. Using aperture-priority, I set f/8 and opt for a low ISO of 200. With this image, shooting handheld allows you more creative freedom than using a tripod.

3 Posing By adopting a low angle and carefully aligning your model with the sun, you will be able to use your subject to obscure the sun's intensity and create an inky black silhouette. However, with Tom standing on the wet, reflective sand and looking out to sea, the result is too static and posed. Overall, the shot is too dark, being at least a stop underexposed.

4 Exposure When shooting backlit subjects, the sun's intensity can fool multi-zone metering patterns into believing the scene is brighter than it is. As a result, the camera selects a faster shutter speed than required, resulting in underexposure. To compensate, I dialled in a stop of positive (+) exposure compensation. I also asked Tom to jump up to add motion to the image.

5 Composition Use trial and error or your camera's histogram to fine-tune the amount of exposure compensation needed. Once you're happy, turn your attention to composition. Props work well when photographing kids and help them to relax in front of the camera. I asked Tom to play catch with a ball, tilting the camera at a slight angle to add energy to the composition.

Final image
The combination of a beautiful sunset and an interesting pose makes for this great image.

✓ Shoot away
When photographing kids playing, set your camera to continuous shooting mode and be prepared to fire sequences of several images

Photographing portraits at home

You don't need expensive equipment or an elaborate set-up to shoot great portraits in the comfort your own home, read on to find out why...

FEW OF US HAVE THE LUXURY of a photography studio and the UK's volatile weather means shooting outdoors is not always an option. But you can still take stunning portraits indoors regardless of a daunting plethora of problems to tackle, such as low light, mixed light, limited space and cluttered backgrounds. In fact, by the end of this guide, you'll recognise more lighting possibilities and know how to make the most of almost any indoor-lighting scenario.

Natural-looking expressions and poses will come easier if you shoot at home where many people feel most relaxed. It's also inexpensive: there's no need to pay for a studio or props, and your basic set-up need only comprise a DSLR or CSC, a portrait lens (a 50mm is ideal), tripod and possibly a flashgun. You can introduce accessories too, such as a reflector or softboxes for your flashguns, but you can always centre your shoot around natural light. Whether you shoot in

your own home or someone else's, go in search of natural light sources and locations. Look for windows and interesting décor, as well as neutral backdrops, white walls and low ceilings to bounce flash off if needed.

There are no rules: the environment dictates the shoot and you have to work with what light you can find or create. If a room is dark in colour, you may need to bring in studio lighting or a flashgun, or decide to work with it for a low-key or low-light portrait. Alternatively, a light-coloured room can act as a giant softbox, bouncing light off the walls.

The time of day and year also offer benefits and challenges. In winter, most natural light will be gone by 3pm, but this means you can turn your hand to low-light portraits instead. In summer, however, there is more natural light available, but it will be much stronger too, so avoid windows in direct sun unless you have heavy diffusion materials handy. The possibilities are endless!

Setting up your digital camera for indoor portraits

1) Exposure Aperture-priority mode is a good place to start when shooting indoor portraits using available light. By using this semi-automatic mode, you'll be able to make the most of limited light by using a wide aperture and shallow depth-of-field to blur distracting backgrounds. If you switch to studioflash, turn your camera to manual and dial in the exposure settings having metered the scene.

2) Metering The multi-zone pattern should be sufficient for an accurate exposure, but if light is limited, make sure your shots are sharp by raising the ISO rating a couple of stops to increase the shutter speed and avoid shake. Also engage image stabilisation and consider using a tripod, although this will limit your mobility a little. It's better to have a sharp image with some noise than one ruined by blur!

3) Focusing While for the most part autofocus will do the job well, it's best to set your camera to central-point focus or to use selective focusing, rather than multi-point AF, as it's likely to pinpoint the nose or eyebrows and not the eyes. Point the central AF point over the eye and half-depress the shutter button to lock focus and then recompose your shot. In very low-light scenarios, you may find that it's easier to switch to manual focus as AF can sometimes struggle in low-contrast situations.

4) White Balance While shooting in Raw means you can tweak the White Balance in Photoshop, it's best to get it right in-camera. Working indoors means you may have to tackle mixed lighting and unflattering colour casts. To correct this, take a spot meter reading off a grey card (or white paper) held in front of your subject's face and use this to set your custom White Balance setting. It will help too if you remember to turn off any indoor lights that are not needed to illuminate the scene, this includes blocking any unneeded window light as this can also vary in temperature depending on the time of day.

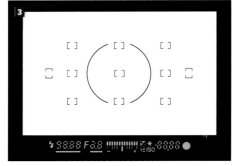

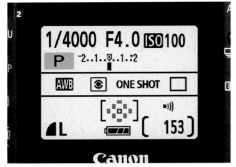

Accessories

Lenses
As light levels can be limited, ideally use a portrait lens with a wide maximum aperture, such as f/1.8, to make the most of the light and create a shallow depth-of-field. A 50mm prime lens or the short end of 55-200mm telezoom are good options. A standard zoom like an 18-55mm kit lens is also usable; the widest focal length is ideal for group shots, but any wider and at close range in cramped spaces you risk distorting perspective.

Reflectors
When there isn't enough light or it's just too harsh, reflectors are invaluable for filling in shadows. The 5-in-1 version is a great tool, with a white side to reflect clean, neutral light, a silver side for a cool, strong light and a gold for a warm golden glow. There is also a black side to absorb light and a diffuser to soften harsh rays. A Lastolite Triflector is also great, with three adjustable sides to control the amount and direction of light.

Flashgun
Your DSLR's built-in flash is suitable for some techniques, but for the most flattering light and more creative options, it's best to invest in a hotshoe-mounted flashgun, which can be triggered off-camera and held at a 45° angle to your model. A flashgun can also be used with accessories like softboxes to make the most of your light without having to invest in a studio set-up.

Flashmeter
When you want to bring some studioflash into the set-up, a flash meter is essential. Attach the sync lead and hold the meter in front of the subject's face, and press the button to find out the aperture you need to input to achieve a correct exposure.

Flashgun diffusion
A burst of off-camera flash could save indoor portraits from being underexposed, but it rarely results in softly-lit, flattering portraits, which is where diffusion accessories come in. The Lastolite Ezybox is brilliant for portraits shot at home; it's portable and easier to prepare and put away than a regular softbox. It comes in two sizes, with the larger version better for photographing groups. Also check out the Strobies Portrait Kit (www.interfitphotographic.com) for more options and the gear section of this guide for other flash accessories,

Dress to impress

Clothing can really add or detract from a shot, so don't make it an afterthought. While you need to judge the right clothes based on the style of the shoot, generally in the autumn or winter opt for block colours, whites and creams to brighten up an image, and darker tones for summer portraits. You may also be surprised at how a checked or stripped top can add to an otherwise simple shot. While there's a time and a place for a man's suit, you may find the best shots come from him taking off his tie and his shoes and undoing his top button for a more relaxed look.

Using available light sources

When natural light is in short supply, household lighting may be your only lifeline. We explain how to work with available light

WHEN YOU'RE SHOOTING indoors, you need to make the most of any available light. This may be in the form of sunlight streaming through a window or patio doors, or artificial lighting like tungsten bulbs.

Covering all the various options to controlling and manipulating daylight indoors could fill a tome, but there are a few basic lighting principles that if applied properly, almost guarantee great results.

The light indoors is usually diffused and non-directional as it bounces off walls, the ceiling and floor, which means it's already flattering for portraits. Should you have strong light streaming in, use net curtains, or hang a sheet of muslin in front of the window to soften the light. Alternatively, move the subject away from the window to soften the light falling on them.

Regardless of the nature of the light or its intensity, the one accessory you should have to hand is a reflector. This lighting aid will help you maximise even the smallest amount of light by bouncing ambient light back on to a subject's face. If you haven't got one already, invest in a silver/white reflector or better still, a 3-in-1 reflector that also includes a gold surface.

If you're struggling for a neutral background, stand your model in front of a window for an instant white backdrop and bounce sunlight back onto the face with a reflector. Alternatively, stand with your back to the window and have the model look out to get an soft, even light over their face or, for more shadow, stand them side on to a window and fill in with a reflector on the opposite side. Usually the bigger the window the softer the light.

At night, available light is limited to artificial home lighting, such as tungsten bulbs, halogen lights built into ceiling panels, spotlights and, in the majority of kitchens, fluorescent lighting. All have very different characteristics in terms of how they distribute light, from focused beams of a spotlight, to the non-directional spread of a tungsten bulb, which should be explored to find the best way they can be used to light the subject effectively. Also, remember that each has its own colour temperature, so be sure to set the appropriate White Balance preset to get accurate colours, or use a test shot of a grey card to set a custom WB setting on your DSLR (your camera's manual will explain how). Another option to try is to use an 'incorrect' White Balance setting to produce images that exhibit a strong cool or warm cast to add mood to the scene. Whichever method you decide to use, we'd recommend you shoot in Raw as you can then easily tweak White Balance when converting images from Raw to JPEG on your computer.

The bathtub 'reflector'!

Unless you have an avocado or pink suite, a bathroom could be the only room in the house where you have access to clean, white light. It can be a great place to maximise natural light as the white surfaces of the walls replicate a similar effect to a giant softbox. If the light is still limited, however, you could try placing your subject in a white bathtub as light will bounce off the sides to mimic the job of a reflector – this technique is ideal for 'little people'. You could also bounce flash off the sides of the tub for a similar effect.

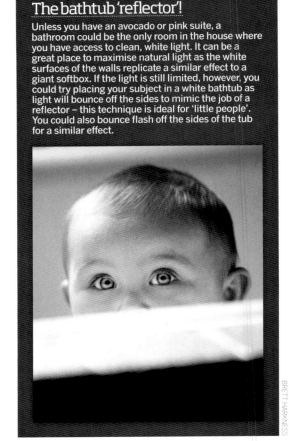

BRETT HARKNESS

BRETT HARKNESS

BRETT HARKNESS

Above: Add mood and mystery
Window light is perfect for flattering portraits. Try adding an air of mystery to your image by having the subject look contemplative while gazing out the window and avoid eye contact. Underexpose the image by -1 or-2 stops to darken the subject a little.

Left: Doing it for the kids!
Be prepared for anything when photographing children. Be ready as soon as you step through the front door, so you don't miss any opportunities to take a candid picture.

Back to a window

For an even light across your model's face, stand with your back to a window and shoot your model facing towards the window light.

Keep it simple and use daylight

Daniel Lezano shows how – with a few little tricks to make the most of the daylight – you can create fantastic lifestyle shots in your own home…

Daniel Lezano MANY LEADING LIFESTYLE portrait photographers use nothing more than ambient daylight for the vast majority of their portrait shoots. So, when we have the benefits of bright, sunny days at our disposal, we should use it to capture some simple yet effective portraits of family and friends. The best thing about shooting lifestyle portraits is that you can do it with the minimum amount of equipment – your DSLR or CSC with a kit lens is enough – although I'm using my favourite optic, the humble (and cheap!) 50mm f/1.8 lens. Due to the unpredictable nature of daylight, lighting aids such as a reflector and a diffuser can come in handy, too, but aren't essential. The key thing to remember is that you want to capture a 'clean' image: in other words, try to keep the subject and the setting as simple as possible. I've opted for the classic combination of having my subject, Bethany, wear a white top and jeans, and shot her lying on my dining room's laminate flooring.

Shoot at a slant

One compositional trick that most lifestyle photographers apply to their images is to slant the camera so that the images are captured with an uneven horizon. This simple technique adds a little energy into the image and is very effective – just take care not to tilt the camera too far.

☑ Focus with care!

You need to ensure your focusing is precise, as using a wide aperture – which gives limited depth-of-field – leaves little margin for error. Select single-point AF, lock the focus on the eye and recompose

My dining room is quite small, so I've had to clear it completely of furniture. As my subject will be lying on the floor, I vacuum it to ensure it's as clean as possible. Due to the cramped space, I open the patio doors in case I need to shoot from the patio. However, I'll start by shooting from within the room and use the white walls as a neutral backdrop. Using a wide aperture to give a shallow depth-of-field is ideal for this type of shot and I'll be trying out my 50mm's maximum aperture of f/1.8, although I'll take most of the images at f/2.5-3.5 as it will improve sharpness.

Diffused daylight

For flattering portraits, the light should be as diffused as possible to avoid your model squinting in direct sunlight or having the light on their face too harsh. In this instance, try to reposition them so they're in the shade or use a diffuser to shade the scene (inset right). If neither of these work, you may need to wait until the sun's position changes or shoot when the sky is more overcast. A silver reflector is handy, even when shooting in non-directional light, to fill in shadows.

1 Test shot My first frame is just to test composition and exposure. I've a clear idea of the type of shot I'm looking to get with Bethany lying down with her lower legs and feet bent back towards her head. This shot isn't bad, but the side-lighting causes her right side to be too dark.

2 Use a reflector I place a silver reflector to Bethany's right, just out of frame, and it makes a noticeable difference; bouncing back enough light to even out the light on her face. The lighting's better, but the wall behind, causes the whole scene to appear a little too cramped for my liking.

Final image
My next shot is perfect and all I need to do is apply minimal post-production. I've boosted the contrast in Curves and cropped the image slightly to give me the result I set out to shoot. Give it a try – you'll be surprised just how easy it is to shoot a great lifestyle portrait at home.

3 Change backgrounds I shift Bethany and my position so that I'm now shooting into the room from the patio. I close the blinds in the room behind to darken the background. The empty space created behind her is an improvement over the original set-up, but my viewpoint is too high.

4 Different viewpoint I crouch down and the lower viewpoint is far better. However, the multi-zone meter has bleached Bethany's face due to the dark background causing it to overexpose the scene. To correct this, I dial in negative exposure compensation. I find -2/3EV is ideal.

Add a warmth to winter images

Find out how to photograph a low-light portrait in front of a log fire

Paul Ward THERE'S NOTHING QUITE like curling up in front of a roaring log fire when it's freezing cold outside.

The fire light elicits a feeling of warmth and comfort, which can also make atmospheric portrait lighting. Unfortunately a fire doesn't throw out as much light as you might think, so you will often have to rely on slow shutter speeds and high ISO ratings. You could use a tripod to reduce the risk of camera shake, but you'll still need to be careful that your subject stays still so not to ruin the shot.

Using a lens with a fast maximum aperture, such as a 50mm f/1.8, helps when shooting in limited light and has the bonus of providing an attractively shallow depth-of-field. Even working with an aperture of f/1.8, you may need to set your ISO to 800 or even 1250 to get a fast enough shutter speed to combat motion blur. Don't go any slower than 1/60sec, otherwise your subject may appear out of focus. Although you'll be working with low-light levels, you can expect quite a lot of contrast in the shot, so using

autofocus should not be a problem. But if you do find the camera struggles to lock focus on the eyes, switch to using manual focus. Bear in mind that when working with a wide aperture like f/1.8, and shallow depth-of-field, you have to be extremely careful to focus in the right place so the image is not rendered out of focus.

There is a fair amount of experimentation involved with this kind of shot, so make sure you have a very cooperative subject and be aware of how hot they can get close to the fire. A log fire is often a point of interest for people so it doesn't look unnatural to have someone gazing into it. If a child can be mesmerised by the flames long enough to sit still you could capture some great portraits, or try positioning a couple in front of the fire with a bottle of wine for a romantic scene instead. Cats and dogs often lie in front of a log fire and can also be perfect subjects for this type of shot. Professional photographer Paul Ward shows us how he created this beautiful atmospheric shot of Megan in her family home using his trusty Canon EOS 50mm f/1.8.

Take steamy portraits outside

An effective way to evoke a sense of warmth in an outdoor winter portrait is to capture a subject bundled in winter clothing clasping a steaming drink. As it's the steam rising from the liquid that gives the photograph atmosphere, you need to find a way to capture it while also lighting your subject well. While you may be able to see the steam clearly, the camera may struggle to pick up the detail. To help with this, position your subject so that the steam is in front of a dark background with the sun behind to help the steam stand out – with a light background the steam probably won't show up at all.

1 Test shot I first did a couple of test shots in aperture-priority mode, with the camera set to f/1.8 to let in the maximum amount of light. I found that to shoot handheld I had to increase the ISO from 640 to 1250 to expose Megan and get a fast enough shutter speed to reduce the risk of motion blur.

2 Use manual mode In aperture-priority, the camera reacts to the changing light on Megan's face, sometimes overexposing it, giving me different results for each shot. Once I had an idea of the best exposure (1/60sec to 1/100sec at f/1.8, ISO 1250), I selected manual mode to get the same results every time.

3 Look at the details Next I tried to see if repositioning Megan on the other side of the fire improved the light on her face. Unfortunately, the natural parting of her hair meant it covered her face, creating shadows. Returning her to the original side, I asked her to tie her hair back to see if it improved the shots.

4 Adjust the colour To enhance the glow, I experimented with the White Balance setting to see if I could make the colour temperature even warmer. To help enhance the atmosphere further, you could try adjusting the Hue/Saturation (*Layer>New Adjustment Layer>Hue/Saturation*) Photoshop.

Final image
This was my favourite image of the shoot. Asking Megan to pull her hair back has allowed the fire light to illuminate her face with minimal shadows. You could get a similar result shooting a portrait by candlelight, if you don't have a log fire.

Fundamentals of flash

If you're looking to take control of your flash photography, the first thing you need to do is discover what flash modes and functions are at your disposal and understand when and how to use them

IN THE PAST, you had the option of two flash modes: on and off. You couldn't really get simpler than that! Today, you've all sorts of modes available that can seem bewildering to beginners and even prove baffling to experienced photographers. What's important for you to remember is that every flash mode has its uses for particular types of subject, so it's essential you know when, as well as how, to use them. The great thing with digital, of course, is that you can try out all the various modes and keep practising until you've got the hang of it. As you'll discover, once you try out each mode in turn, you'll soon learn what it's best for and how you can make the most of it. We've set out the guide to cover all the more straightforward flash modes first and will cover the more creative options later. We've also provided essential information panels that cover flash terminology and useful accessories to help you make the most of your flashgun.

Why you need to buy a dedicated flashgun

Almost all digital SLRs have an integral flashgun, while most CSCs have either a built-in flash or a clip-on unit supplied with the camera. So why buy an additional unit? There are several reasons why, but here are the three main advantages of using a dedicated flashgun:

Power: The output from a built-in flash is good enough for shooting subjects within a couple of metres' range, but won't extend further. Hotshoe-mounted flashguns are far more powerful, allowing you to expose subjects several metres away.

Features: Your built-in flash has several modes on offer, but can't match the sophistication of a separate unit. As well as the bounce head, there are additional modes on offer that allow for more creative flash photography.

Flexibility: The fact you can use a dedicated flashgun off-camera opens up a wealth of possibilities. You can also combine several flashguns for a multiple lighting set-up to rival what's possible from a studioflash system, but in a far more portable outfit.

Anatomy panel: Know your way around a flashgun...

1) Flash head: Your flash head will most likely angle vertically and horizontally: an action commonly referred to as bounce and swivel actions. Most flashguns have a zoom head, where the light coverage changes to suit the lens in use to optimise the range.

2) AF assist lamp: In low light, you may see a red patterned beam emitted by the flashgun to help the camera lock focus.

3) Built-in diffuser/ reflector: Slide out the diffuser and drop it in place over the flash window to soften the light, or use the reflector to redirect some of the flash output.

4) External power socket: Many mid- to top-end flashgun models accept an external power source.

5) LCD monitor: The sophistication of its features means that many flashguns have an LCD panel offering a wealth of information about what modes have been selected, as well as a flash-distance scale to give you a visual representation of the flash range at your current chosen settings.

6) Control buttons: The advanced features on flashguns mean there are a large number of buttons, with most controlling more than one function. You're advised to spend a little time getting used to the layout, as they're not always straightforward to use.

7) Hotshoe fitting: The hotshoe fitting has pins that touch contacts on the camera's hotshoe to communicate information and trigger the flash when the shutter is released. All DSLR hotshoes follow the same design, with the exception of Sony's Alpha series. Some CSCs have accessory shoes, while others lack this facility.

8) Ready/test lamp: Most models have a two-stage lamp that lights green then red to indicate partial and full charge. With many, you can press this lamp to test-fire the flash.

9) Locking mechanism: This facility prevents your flash slipping off the hotshoe by locking it in place.

10) Stand: Many flashguns that sport a wireless facility come supplied with a stand that allows the flashgun to be positioned, ready for use off-camera. An alternative is to buy a ball & socket tripod head, like the £25 Cullmann CB2 (www.newprouk.co.uk), which allows you to precisely position the flashgun while mounted on a lighting stand or tripod.

AF assist

Some DSLRs have an AF assist lamp on the body, but this is overridden by the AF assist on a flashgun as it has a better range

Common flash terms explained

●**TTL flash metering:** Your camera uses Through The Lens (TTL) metering to ensure accurate exposures. Most cameras use the multi-zone pattern as the basis for exposure calculation, with some offering the option via a Custom Function to switch to using centre-weighted metering. Some systems fire a 'pre-flash' to aid exposures and others even boast a Flash-Exposure Lock (FE-Lock) facility that allows you to take a spot reading using flash when shooting in particularly tricky shooting situations. For the vast majority of pictures, you can rely on the standard TTL system to give good results.

●**Red-eye:** We've all experienced red-eye in our flash photos – the red you see is the reflection of the flash off the blood vessels in the retinas at the back of the eyes. If the red-eye reduction mode of the camera doesn't work, you can easily reduce or remove the problem using one or the techniques covered later in this guide.

●**Flash-sync speed:** Your camera has a shutter speed at which it synchronises with the flash, usually between 1/90sec and 1/250sec. You can select a shutter speed slower than this, but not one faster, as this can lead to part of your image appearing black.

●**Guide Number:** The Guide Number (GN) is an indication of the flashgun's power: the higher the Guide Number, the more powerful it is. It's often stated as a number followed by (ISO 100, m), which is an indication of its power in metres when used at a particular ISO setting. It's rare that you'll be required to calculate a flash exposure, but if you do, set the camera to manual, the shutter speed to its sync speed and calculate the exposure with this simple formula: Aperture = Guide Number / subject-to-flash distance. So, if your subject is ten metres from the flash and your Guide Number is 40, you need to set an aperture of f/4. Most built-in units have a GN of around 12, while most dedicated flashguns vary from 28 to over 50!

●**Master and slave flash:** If you're using a multiple flash set-up, you'll use a 'Master' flashgun to control the 'Slave' flashguns. A switch on the back of the flashguns allows you to set them to either setting.

●**Flash coverage:** This indicates the spread of light from the flash. It's stated as a focal length (usually around 18mm), so that you're aware that if you use a lens wider than the stated figure, you risk dark corners/edges to your image due a lack of flash coverage.

Flashtastic! Learning to use flash properly can help you capture dazzling results like this.

BRETT HARKNESS

Where to find flash control settings on your digital camera

Most cameras have a flash button on the body and further options in their menu system, here's examples of how to access the features

Canon
Press the flash button to pop up the flash. The Flash Control setting on the menu's first tab allows the mode to be set.

Nikon
With some models, press and hold the flash button. You can also access via the MENU and via the i button if available on your camera.

Olympus
Press the flash mode button, make your selection using the four-way control or the input dial, then press OK.

Panasonic
Press MENU and scroll through options in the Rec tab. If your camera has a Q Menu, you can add flash modes as a shortcut.

Pentax
Press the flash button and use the four-way control to choose a mode. Set flash exposure compensation via the input dial.

Samsung
Press MENU and scroll through options in the Camera tab. Alternatively, press Fn and select a mode with the four-way control.

Sony
Press the flash mode button, make your selection using the four-way control or the input dial, then press OK.

Flash accessories

There are various accessories that can be used with your camera's flash and these can be split into the following main categories:

Lighting aids: There are a wealth of softboxes, diffusers, brollies, beauty dishes and other lighting aids available to help soften or direct the output from your dedicated flashgun. They vary in price from under £20 for a simple diffuser to up to £200 for a decent softbox. We recommend you check out the following:

● Diffuser: Stofen Omni-bounce £17; www.newprouk.com

● Softbox: Lastolite Ezybox (38cm) £170; www.lastolite.com

● Beauty dish: Speedlight Pro £70; www.speedlightprokit.co.uk

● Complete kit: Interfit Strobies £120; www.interfitphotographic.com

Brackets: These hold your flash to the side of your camera, rather than have it mounted on your hotshoe, which improves the lighting effect and frees your hotshoe for dedicated accessories like a remote trigger. Check out the range by Custom Brackets (www.flaghead.co.uk).

Off-camera triggers or leads: If you want to use your flashgun off-camera, you'll need these to retain dedication with your flash (unless they have a built-in wireless trigger). Manufacturers have their own, but Hama (www.hama.co.uk) Hahnel (www.hahnel.ie) and Phottix (www.intro2020.co.uk) offer affordable options.

Gels: Slip a coloured gel over the flashhead and you can bathe the scene in colour. Many pros use it with an off-camera flash to illuminate a backdrop. Honl (www.flaghead.co.uk) and Hama (www.hama.co.uk) offer excellent flash gel sets.

Battery packs: If you regularly shoot lots of flash exposures (for instance, at weddings), then a battery pack is a cost-effective option and an alternative to AA rechargeable batteries. Quantum (www.flaghead.co.uk) is the most popular brand.

Slave cell: Pop one on the bottom of a flash and it will fire when the sensor detects a flash output. If you have non-dedicated manual flashguns, it's an inexpensive way of using multiple flash set-ups. Hama's Slave cell costs £20.

Ball & socket flash platform: If you use the flash off-camera, you'll need a 'foot' to stand it on a surface or a ball & socket head with a flash-compatible platform bracket to hold it securely. Cullmann (www.newprouk.com), 9 (www.interfitphotographic.com) and other independent brands have several options. For more of our recommended flash accessories see p144-145.

Basic flash modes

Auto: DSLRs don't have an Auto-flash mode as such, but rather have certain exposure modes that pop up the flash automatically. Some CSCs do have an Auto setting among their flash modes and this works much like it does on a compact camera, firing the flash when needed in low light and taking pictures without in brighter conditions.

When to use Auto flash

● Leaving your flash set to Auto mode makes sense when shooting general snapshots indoors as it's most likely that shooting using ambient light only may result in camera shake ruining images.

Forced-on (fill-in): You don't have to wait for the camera to suggest you need to use the flash – you can pop it up yourself by pressing the flash button. Do this to add a touch of fill-in flash to remove shadows and add catchlights to daylight portraits, or when your subject's face is in shadow. The amount of fill-in flash is determined automatically by the camera, but you can boost or reduce it using flash exposure compensation (explained over the page).

When to use fill-in flash

● The subject is standing with their back to the sun, so fill-in flash is used to reveal detail.

● Your subject is positioned under a tree with dappled shadows across the face.

Flash-off: This mode isn't found on the majority of SLRs, as there is no auto pop-up flash facility unless the camera is set to a scene mode where it decides if the flash is needed or not. However, it does exist on some DSLRs as a mode on the mode dial and is designed to be used to prevent accidentally firing the flash in locations where flash photography is not allowed, such as museums or theatres. This mode is found on all CSCs, regardless of whether or not it has an integral flash.

When to turn the flash off

● When shooting through glass, leave the flash off to avoid reflections

● In locations where flash is not permitted, ensure it's switched off.

Red-eye reduction: If you're shooting indoor portraits using the camera's built-in flash and there is very little available light, then you run the risk of the subjects suffering from red-eye. Using this mode sets the flash to fire either a fast burst of 'strobe' flashes or a constant beam of light, with the aim of closing your subject's pupils and reducing the risk of red-eye. As well as this mode, you can minimise the problem of red-eye by using one of the following techniques:

● **Use bounce flash:** Red-eye is the result of direct flash, so bounce flash instantly removes the problem (see panel opposite).

● **Move the flash away from the lens:** The risk of red-eye decreases the further the flash is away from the lens. A hotshoe-mounted flash is less likely to result in red-eye, while red-eye is extremely rare when the flash is off-camera.

● **Avoid alcohol:** Alcohol leads to pupils dilating so your subjects are more likely to have red-eye if they've already started drinking!

Red-eye reduction OFF

Red-eye reduction ON

● **Increase ambient light:** If you're using the built-in flash, the previous points won't apply. The best option is to switch on the room lights or shoot in a brighter room, as the higher the ambient light, the smaller the subject's pupils.

● **Cheat!** If all else fails, use software to remove red-eye from your images. Many packages have a red-eye function that can be used to automatically remove the problem. It's also found on some cameras, too!

Using bounce flash

The light from your flash can be unforgiving for portraits, which is why most hotshoe-mounted flashguns boast a bounce head. In its standard position, the flash head delivers direct flash at your subject, which gives a less than flattering effect as well as producing shadows behind the subject. By bouncing flash off a ceiling or wall, it is more evenly spread to give a better result, while also eliminating the problem of shadows. You don't have to worry about the exposure – the camera takes care of this for you. What you do have to be careful with is how much you angle the head – you want to aim it to bounce off the surface halfway between you and the subject – aim the head too low and the flash will bounce behind the subject; raise it too far and it will fall in front of them. Also make sure you bounce it off a white or neutral-coloured surface –the flash will take on the colour of the surface, so bounce it off a red wall and it will bathe your subject in a red cast. If you have a flashgun with a built-in reflector or diffuser, use it to further improve the flash effect.

DIRECT FLASH

BOUNCE FLASH

BOUNCE WITH REFLECTOR

Choosing the correct exposure mode to use with flash

While the TTL flash exposure system on your camera will aim to give you perfectly exposed images every time, it's worth noting that the actual result varies depending on the exposure mode the camera is set to. How this works depends on the camera brand and model, but our easy reference table provides information on how using flash with each of the core creative modes affects how the image is captured.

Brand	Canon	Nikon	Pentax	Olympus	Sony
Program	Camera sets shutter speed and aperture, but raises shutter speed to avoid camera shake. The background may be dark.	Camera sets exposure, but raises shutter speed to avoid camera shake, unless slow-sync mode is set. Background may be dark.	Camera sets exposure, but raises shutter speed to avoid camera shake, unless slow-sync mode is set. Background may be dark.	Camera sets exposure, but raises shutter speed to avoid camera shake, unless slow-sync mode is set. Background may be dark.	Camera sets exposure, but raises shutter speed to avoid camera shake, unless slow-sync mode is set. Background may be dark.
Aperture-priority	User picks aperture; camera calculates flash exposure accordingly. Shutter speed is picked to render ambient light correctly. Be aware of camera shake.	User picks the aperture and the camera selects flash exposure accordingly. Shutter speed is limited to prevent camera shake, unless slow-sync mode is selected.	User sets aperture and camera sets shutter speed to correctly expose background, up to the maximum sync speed. Risk of camera shake in low light.	User picks aperture and camera selects flash exposure accordingly. Shutter speed limited to prevent camera shake, unless slow-sync mode is also selected.	User picks aperture and camera selects flash exposure accordingly. Shutter speed limited to prevent camera shake, unless slow-sync mode is also selected.
Shutter-priority	User picks shutter speed and camera picks corresponding aperture for ambient light, then calculates flash output according to this aperture.	User picks shutter speed and camera picks corresponding aperture to expose ambient light correctly, then calculates flash output according to this aperture.	User picks shutter speed and camera picks corresponding aperture to expose ambient light properly, then calculates flash output according to this aperture.	User picks shutter speed and camera picks corresponding aperture to expose ambient light correctly, then calculates flash output according to this aperture.	User picks shutter speed and camera picks corresponding aperture to expose ambient light correctly, then calculates flash output according to this aperture.
Manual	You set the aperture and shutter speed (at or below the flash sync) to ensure the scene receives enough ambient light. The TTL flash system ensures the subject is correctly exposed.	You set the aperture and shutter speed (at or below the flash sync) to ensure the scene receives enough ambient light. The TTL flash system ensures the subject is correctly exposed.	You set the aperture and shutter speed (at or below the flash sync) to ensure the scene receives enough ambient light. The TTL flash system ensures the subject is correctly exposed.	You set the aperture and shutter speed (at or below the flash sync) to ensure the scene receives enough ambient light. The TTL flash system ensures the subject is correctly exposed.	You set the aperture and shutter speed (at or below the flash sync) to ensure the scene receives enough ambient light. The TTL flash system ensures the subject is correctly exposed.
Exposure compensation	Affects ambient light exposure only.	Affects ambient and flash exposure.	Affects ambient and flash exposure.	Affects ambient light exposure only.	Affects ambient and flash exposure.
Flash exposure compensation	Affects flash exposure only.	Affects flash exposure only.	Affects flash exposure only.	Affects flash exposure only.	Affects flash exposure only.

* Please note that the stated information relates to most general shooting conditions. However, in certain situations, the camera and flash will operate differently.

Creative flash modes

Second (rear) curtain sync: Your camera is normally set up for first-curtain flash synchronisation, which means that when you take a picture, the burst of flash is at the start of the exposure. With most standard exposures, this system works well, but when using a longer exposure, it can adversely affect the result if there is a subject moving in the frame. What happens is that the burst of flash when you first press the shutter records the subject in its original position, but as it continues to move through the frame, it records a 'streak' across the picture. To make the image more natural, select second-curtain sync (also known as rear-curtain sync) to fire the flash at the end of the exposure. The problem with second-curtain sync is that when shooting a moving subject, you never quite know where it will be in the frame when the flash fires. This isn't an issue if the shutter speed is reasonably quick, such as 1/8sec, but it can present a problem if you're using a very slow shutter speed, especially if the subject is moving quickly.

When to use second-curtain sync flash
- When you're shooting moving subjects with a slower shutter speed to reveal motion.

Slow-sync: This mode involves combining flash with a slow shutter speed. The longer exposure time allows ambient light to be recorded in the scene, while the flash takes care of the main subject. With the standard flash setting, the camera uses a faster shutter speed to ensure there is no camera shake, but the result is that, while the subject is well exposed, the background is very dark. Because of the length the shutter remains open, you should place the camera on a tripod to ensure the image isn't spoilt by movement during the exposure. That said, you can capture creative results by purposely moving the camera during the exposure – try rotating the camera clockwise or anti-clockwise and note how bright hotspots of light record as streaks. Many cameras have a slow-sync mode that you select, while others automatically set the flash to slow-sync when you use particular exposure modes – check your camera's instruction manual. Finally, it's worth noting that, with some cameras, you can combine slow-sync flash with second-curtain sync.

When to use slow-sync flash
- Use slow-sync to reveal ambient light in the background and a flash-exposed subject.
- The relatively slow shutter speed creates unusual effects when moving the camera.

Wireless flash: This facility allows you to fire off-camera flash without the need for any form of wired connection, giving you freedom to experiment with flash. The actual procedure for shooting wirelessly varies from brand to brand, but the basic set-up involves setting your camera to Wireless flash mode and using the integral or hotshoe-mounted flash to set off the off-camera 'slave' flashguns. Wireless flash photography is possible even if your camera lacks a Wireless mode by attaching a wireless trigger to the hotshoe, with a transmitter fitted to the base of your off-camera flash. Branded triggers are expensive, so a far more affordable option is an independent trigger. You can opt for the least expensive triggers, which do not provide TTL flash metering, or more expensive options that give full dedication. The latter option is the best choice for most people, but if you're using older non-dedicated flashguns at manual power settings, the cheaper option is suitable. Our favourite flash triggers include the Hahnel Combi RF Interfit Titan Pro and Pocket Wizards are the brands to look if you're serious about multiple off-camera flash photography.

When to use wireless flash
- Multiple flash set-ups or when using a colour gel on an off-camera flash to liven up a backdrop.

FP/High Speed flash: This mode is available on a limited number of cameras and flashguns and allows the flash to be used at any shutter speed, therefore not restricting it to the standard flash-sync speed. This is particularly useful for sports photographers looking to use flash in bright daylight to freeze action and it's also popular with lifestyle photographers looking to combine flash with wide apertures in bright daylight. It's a highly sophisticated mode suited for specialist rather than general photography.

When to use high-speed flash
- Using flash to freeze action in daylight.
- When you want to use flash in bright daylight.

Manual power settings: Many hotshoe-mounted flashguns, as well as a small number of Compact System Cameras, boast manual power settings. These are set to fire the flash at particular power ratios, in steps from full power to ½-power to ¼-power etc, down to $\frac{1}{64}$-power or lower. When used at a manual power setting, the flash output will be consistent, regardless of the camera settings, ambient light or any other variable, so set it to ¼- or ½-power and it will fire the same output every time. This means that, once set up, the flash exposures are consistent – this is useful if you're photographing a variety of subjects that range from dark to light, or are highly reflective. Once you've set the manual power ratio of your flash(es) to give a decent exposure, so long as you don't vary the flash-to-subject distance, every exposure will be consistent. Another instance where manual flash settings is useful is if your flashgun is very old or a different brand from your camera. By using it in manual mode, with either a trigger or a slave cell attached to the mount at the base of the flash, you're able to shoot using a multiple flash set-up. Manual power is also ideal when you want to paint a scene with flash, as shown here.

Creative flash control

Flash Exposure Compensation (FEC)

This isn't a function that you may use too often, but it's important, as it provides you with a fast and easy way to control the level of flash output. In the same way that you use exposure compensation to add or subtract from the exposure that the camera has determined is correct, FEC is used to boost or reduce the amount of flash the camera has decided is required. You'll usually want to do this after reviewing an image you've just taken, having decided you'd prefer a little more or less flash. Most often, this is when you've taken a shot using fill-in flash and decided that the flash/ambient light balance isn't quite right. However, with some brands of camera, including Nikon, Pentax and Sony, adjustments made using exposure compensation also affect the flash exposure, so FEC can be applied to compensate for this.

External flash func. setting

Flash exp. comp   ⁻2 . 1 . 0 . 1 . ⁺2

DISP. Clear flash settings

No FEC applied

-1EV FEC applied

Flash control

The camera's flash output was too strong for our taste, so reducing it one stop using FEC gave a more natural result.

Simulate low evening sunlight

Learn how to use off-camera flash to create attractive hairlight

WHEN USING FLASH to light a portrait, most photographers point it at the subject's face, but by placing it behind the model's head you can create attractive hairlight – adding a different dimension to the image. It's a great creative technique to try in the winter months too, when you don't fancy going outdoors but want to simulate the look of a low evening sun from the warmth of your home.

To get the best results, the subject should ideally have curly or wavy hair, and be placed in front of a dark background to accentuate the light. You'll also need to experiment with your flash's power to find a balance between overpowering the ambient light and getting the right spread through the hair. For instance, if you're doing a full-body portrait, a burst of flash at ½ power would work best, while a head shot might require only ¼ power. Play with the distance of your flash to your subject's head as well, but make sure the flash is completely hidden so it diffuses through the hair. Also consider your aperture: minimal depth-of-field will soften the spread of light while a narrow aperture will produce a star-like effect from the flash.

Reflectors

You can use your camera's integral flash unit to illuminate the face, or you could use a reflector instead to bounce some light onto the subject's face. You can control the tone of the light by the choice of your reflector too. If you want a cool tone, opt for a silver reflector, or for a warm cast, try a gold reflector. Alternatively, why not try Lastolite's TriGrip Sunfire or Sunlite reflector, like we've used in this step-by-step, as it has strips of silver and gold for a more natural cast. If you only have a silver or gold reflector, you could always experiment with your image's White Balance in camera or Adobe Camera Raw to warm it up or cool the tone down.

Backlighting a portrait with flash

Professional lifestyle photographer Brett Harkness frequently uses his off-camera flash behind his subjects, whether to create a dramatic burst of light behind a full-body portrait or to add a subtle, attractive hairlight to a head shot. He shows us how…

Without reflector

With reflector

1 (Above) Use natural light To start with, we position Emma in a doorway so we can use natural light to fill in the shadows on her face. During the winter months, however, when light levels are low you may need to use a reflector or a second flash to light her face, held approximately three or four feet away so not to overpower the backlight. With the camera and flash set to manual, I dial in f/5.6 and ISO 500, because of the relatively low light, and place the flashgun on the step behind Emma.

2 (Right) Take test shots I take my first shot of Emma at f/5.6 with the flash behind her set to ⅛ power and no reflector. The flash isn't strong enough and her face is underexposed. So I set the flash to ¼ power and ask my assistant to hold a reflector a few feet away from Emma's face to fill in the shadows.

3 (Left) Tidy the background As I can see the stairs in the background of the pictures, I add a blanket over the steps to get rid of the white line and darken the background to enhance the backlight.

4 (Above) Try different WB settings You may also want to try playing with your camera's White Balance settings to see what effect it has on the picture. Normally if you're working with flash, you would set Flash or Custom WB, but why not try Daylight or Tungsten to alter the tone of the image? Alternatively, you could shoot in Raw and play with the WB in post-production.

Final image
With slight tweaks to the contrast in Photoshop and a little skin softening, we're left with a beautiful portrait.

How to add drama to sky for outdoor portraits

Underexposing the scene and using flash to light the subject is a great way to add impact to portraits

MORE OFTEN THAN NOT, flash is used to balance flash and ambient lighting, or to fill in shadows, but now and again, it pays to use flash to overpower the ambient light and completely transform a scene.

A great technique to try is to capture a dramatic sky by underexposing the scene, leading it to appear far darker than it does in reality, while allowing the flash to correctly expose the subject. You can do it two ways: use the exposure compensation facility to dial in a negative value, or work in manual mode, both of which we'll explain in further detail.

Regardless of which you choose, for the best results, avoid using the camera's integral flash or mounting a flash on the hotshoe and instead trigger a remote flash via a slave or off-camera flash cord. Simply reposition the flash to the side of the subject to immediately change the function of the flash from a flat fill-in light to one that's directional and contrast-enhancing. For the purpose of this step-by-step, we'll explain how to do this technique using manual settings rather than relying on your camera's TTL system, as it offers greater control and a chance to learn and experiment.

Different camera and flash systems work in different ways, so if you do want to try the exposure compensation method with TTL, check your camera's instruction manual.

Remember: when working with manual flash, the shutter speed controls the amount of ambient light reaching the sensor, while aperture controls flash output. For this technique, shutter speed is paramount as you're exposing for the sky, not the subject. The faster the shutter speed, the darker the ambience will be; the slower the shutter speed, the more you encourage the influence of ambient light.

Using radio triggers

Most of the time, once a flash is off-camera and triggered by a radio release it loses its TTL capabilities, so it's important your flash has manual settings. To retain TTL, you could opt for a dedicated off-camera lead, but you will be restricted by the length of the cord. However, if you're comfortable using manual flash, the more affordable option is a slave cell (see p56) or a flash remote trigger – there are many available, varying in price and functions. While PocketWizards are brilliant, and a market leader for performance, they're also expensive. Camera manufacturers also have their own remotes but we'd recommend independent versions by the likes of Calumet, Kenro, Hahnel and Seculine as they're cheaper and do the job well enough. The Hahnel Combi TF, for instance, is a bargain at around £60 and doubles up as a remote flash trigger and shutter release. Seculine's highly-efficient Twin Link T2D Wireless Radio Flash Trigger Kit can be bought for around £120. Regardless of what remote you buy, remember you need a transmitter to sit on your camera's hotshoe and a receiver to attach to each of your off-camera flashguns for it to work.

Using exposure compensation

Instead of using manual mode, set your camera to aperture-priority mode, your flash to TTL and meter for the background. Dial in the aperture you want and then set a negative value on the camera's exposure compensation to at least two stops to underexpose the scene: the flash will take care of the subject. If you're shooting with a Nikon, you may have to increase your flash exposure compensation by two stops too, as the flash and exposure compensation are linked. Have a play and experiment with results.

Getting a dramatic sky with an outdoor portrait

This is an advanced technique, so requires practice. Pro photographer Brett Harkness, who regularly uses it, explains how to make the most of manual flash and moody skies. On this shoot, it's overcast and there's a mass of detail in the sky to capture. As Brett likes his shots sharp front-to-back, he uses a small aperture of around f/13 and sets his flash to ¼ power to compensate. If you want shallow depth-of-field, keep the flash close to your subject, set the flash to ⅛ power and open the aperture.

1 **(Above) Prepare the flash** I ask my assistant to hold the flashgun several feet away from the model, Emma. Because we're not using any diffusion accessories, I have him hold the flash vertically to get a bigger spread of light over her. Sunglasses and gold fabric add a fashion-shoot feel.

2 **(Right) Underexpose the scene** To capture a moody sky, I have to dramatically underexpose the scene using a fast shutter speed to retain detail in the sky. As you can see, a fast shutter speed has underexposed the scene, but without using flash it means the subject is also very dark.

3 **(Left) Set exposure** Once I start using flash, my shutter speed is immediately limited to the camera's sync speed – in this case 1/250sec. With my camera set to manual, I set the aperture that gives the scene the correct exposure for the ambient light. I then set the flashgun to ¼ power, which exposes Emma well, but the scene lacks drama and mood.

4 **(Below) Raise the flash** To improve the effect, my assistant raises the flash and points it down on Emma. However, the key to darkening the scene behind her is to close down the aperture (in this instance by two stops) so that the background is underexposed, resulting in a far moodier result.

Final image
With a few tweaks to
the Curves and Levels
in Photoshop, Brett's
produced a dramatic
portrait with a single
off-camera flash.
Give it a go!

Add colour with flash gels

Give your portrait more impact with a simple wireless flash technique

Daniel Lezano GETTING TO USE only one flashgun proves a daunting prospect for many, so how does the thought of using two grab you? This technique deals with showing you how to light a subject with one flashgun, while a second flash is used to illuminate the background. It's a useful technique when you want to highlight detail in the scene or, as shown here, you want to use flash gels to light it in a different colour.

While the technique may sound incredibly difficult, it's actually quite easy to achieve. You need to use your camera's integral flash (or a hotshoe-mounted flashgun) to illuminate your subject, which is pretty straightforward as the exposure is taken care of automatically by the camera thanks to the wonders of TTL metering. A second flashgun is triggered automatically by the main flash to illuminate the background, so you've little to do other than ensure that the remote flash is set up correctly, which as the panel on the right reveals, is pretty easy to do. And, if you think this sounds expensive, it isn't, with several independent brands like Hahnel, Seculine, Phottix and Interfit offering very affordable options.

Flash gels are essentially small sheets of coloured plastic that are placed over the flash head to colour the flash output. The flash gel is held in place over the head using Velcro or an elastic band, and with a number of kits available in a choice of colours, it's an inexpensive and easy way to add creative flash effects to your images. Incidentally, larger flash gel kits are available that can be used with studioflash heads too, and, in fact, the technique we've used here can easily be applied to studioflash set-ups as well as flashguns.

Using flash gels to illuminate a background is equally suited to both indoor and outdoor locations. Plain backdrops as well as textured surfaces are suitable, although the latter does provide additional visual interest. It's also worth bearing in mind that you can use more than one flashgun for the background, so feel free to mix colour gels. The key is to experiment as much as possible, as this is when creative photos present themselves.

Remote flashgun set-up

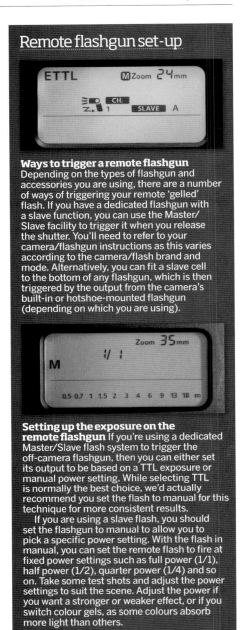

Ways to trigger a remote flashgun
Depending on the types of flashgun and accessories you are using, there are a number of ways of triggering your remote 'gelled' flash. If you have a dedicated flashgun with a slave function, you can use the Master/Slave facility to trigger it when you release the shutter. You'll need to refer to your camera/flashgun instructions as this varies according to the camera/flash brand and mode. Alternatively, you can fit a slave cell to the bottom of any flashgun, which is then triggered by the output from the camera's built-in or hotshoe-mounted flashgun (depending on which you are using).

Setting up the exposure on the remote flashgun If you're using a dedicated Master/Slave flash system to trigger the off-camera flashgun, then you can either set its output to be based on a TTL exposure or manual power setting. While selecting TTL is normally the best choice, we'd actually recommend you set the flash to manual for this technique for more consistent results.

If you are using a slave flash, you should set the flashgun to manual to allow you to pick a specific power setting. With the flash in manual, you can set the remote flash to fire at fixed power settings such as full power (1/1), half power (1/2), quarter power (1/4) and so on. Take some test shots and adjust the power settings to suit the scene. Adjust the power if you want a stronger or weaker effect, or if you switch colour gels, as some colours absorb more light than others.

1 Just flash Here's my subject photographed using just a hotshoe-mounted flashgun. She's well exposed but the background is drab and dark.

2 Light the background I've set up a remote flashgun behind her, which fires to light the wall in the background but the effect isn't attractive.

3 Add a flash gel I fitted a Lumiquest red gel – the colour adds interest but, with the remote flash set to TTL, its output isn't as strong as we'd like.

4 Use full-power Setting the remote flash to manual power provides a far stronger output, although the full-power 1/1 setting is far too strong.

5 Play with the settings I try various manual power settings to see which provides the best result and find that half-power works best here.

Final image
While the red gel is attractive, it's overpowering, so I try other colours and find green works the best.

Studioflash outfits

Some newcomers find studioflash intimidating, but the truth is, using it isn't as difficult as you think

ALTHOUGH THERE ARE VARIOUS studioflash kits available, ranging in price from under £200 to thousands, most of them have very similar features and all follow basic principles of operation. A studioflash head is designed to fire a burst of flash at a given power setting – the extra functions and accessories are all geared to allow the photographer more control of the flash output. Truly mastering a studioflash system can take years but, thankfully, getting to grips with the essentials is relatively easy. Much like using ambient light, the key factor to success is learning how to control the flash output so your subject is lit the way you'd like it to be. The big difference between studio and ambient light is your level of control – you are able to fine-tune the lighting's intensity and direction, as well as the nature of the light falling on the subject, far more accurately than you could ever achieve with natural light. This makes it an incredibly versatile form of lighting but, obviously, one that does take time to learn to use accurately. Here, we cover the basic workings of studioflash and how the various attachments, such as softboxes and brollies, can be used to control how your subject is lit.

Anatomy of a studioflash head

This illustration is of the rear of an Interfit head, but most brands will have a similar layout, with easy-to-use and well labelled controls.

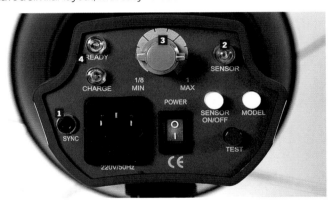

Rear of light
You'll normally find controls on the rear of the head, but some models have them on the side, too.

1) Sync socket: Most studioflash outfits are supplied with a sync lead, which connects your camera to your flash head, to allow the flash to fire when you press the shutter button.

2) Slave cell: This sensor detects any flash output, so if your camera is connected to one light in a multiple set-up, its output will trigger the slave cell on other lights, making them fire together.

3) Power settings: A key function of studioflash heads is being able to adjust the power output. Basic heads have fixed settings, eg ¼ power, ½ power and so on, while advanced heads have stepless variable settings.

4) Status lights/beeps: Many heads have lights that indicate when the head has sufficient charge to fire.

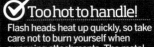

Too hot to handle!
Flash heads heat up quickly, so take care not to burn yourself when swapping attachments. The metal mount, as well as the bulb, can get hot, especially when the modelling lamp is turned on

Front of light
Removing the lighting attachment will usually reveal two bulbs, each with different uses.

5) Modelling lamp: This tungsten bulb remains switched on to allow you to compose the image, focus on the subject and to assess the lighting effect.

6) Flash bulb: These provide the powerful flash output. Most brands have specialised bulbs to fit certain heads or studioflash series. They're very fragile, so handle them with utmost care.

Setting up your camera for using studioflash

Set the camera to manual and the correct flash sync speed. Then fit a PC adaptor to your hotshoe to connect to the flash sync lead

CANON EOS DSLRS
(1) Set the main control dial to M to select manual mode
(2) Turn the input dial behind the shutter button and set the flash sync speed
(3) Once you've taken a flashmeter reading, press and hold down the +/- button, then turn the input dial to set the aperture you require

MOST NIKON DSLRS
(1) Set the main control dial to M to select manual mode
(2) Turn the input dial behind the shutter button and set the flash sync speed
(3) Once you've taken a flashmeter reading, turn the input dial on the front of the handgrip to set the aperture

PENTAX K-SERIES DSLRS
(1) Set the main control dial on the top-plate to M to select manual mode
(2) Turn the input dial behind the shutter button and set the flash sync speed
(3) Once you've taken a flashmeter reading, press and hold down the +/- button, then turn the input dial to set the aperture you require

SONY ALPHA DSLRS
(1) Set the main control dial on the top-plate to Tv to select shutter-priority mode
(2) Turn the input dial in front of the shutter button and set the flash sync speed
(3) Once you've taken a flashmeter reading, press and hold down the +/- button, then turn the input dial to set the aperture you require

COMPACT SYSTEM CAMERAS
Very few CSCs sport the exposure mode dial found on the majority of digital SLRs, but it's still very easy to select the exposure mode. With most models all you need to do is press the Menu button or the four-way control dial to display the exposure modes and rotate the wheel to M to select manual mode. With touchscreen models, simply press the M icon on the screen.

Studioflash accessories

Get the best out of your flash system with lighting attachments and accessories

STUDIOFLASH HEADS ARE DESIGNED to produce a high-power burst of light, but it's the lighting attachment you use that dictates the effect of the flash on the subject. If you've ever looked into buying a studioflash system, you'll no doubt have seen various types of attachments available, each having their own way of affecting the intensity and nature of light. While most basic kits are often supplied with a brolly or two and 'spills', there are a huge number of optional accessories available and getting to know which are best suited to your needs is important. In our comparison set below, we have used the most typical types of attachments available for most studioflash kits to give you an idea of how each affects the light.

As well as lighting attachments, other accessories can play a big part in the quality of your final results, or just make the process a lot easier.

For instance, a flash meter is useful to identify the correct aperture you need to set your camera to for a perfect exposure, and a remote trigger is also handy. Which background you use also affects the final image: there are a variety available, from plain to coloured patterns, to paper rolls that fit on frames and collapsible backdrops. A reflector should not be overlooked either; it bounces light back onto the subject or background as an alternative to using an additional light. Silver is the most efficient, white provides a softer and more natural effect, while a black reflector can accentuate cheekbones! For further details on these accessories, visit our *Portrait Kit* guide section.

Flashmeter readings
When using studioflash, make sure the white dome (invercone) on your flashmeter is set over the sensor, so that it takes incident light readings, which will prove to be the most accurate

Umbrella (brolly)
Available in white, silver and translucent, a brolly is one of the cheapest accessories available. Silver is very efficient at bouncing light, white gives a soft, natural effect, while translucent brollies provide the most diffused light.

Softbox
A real favourite, as it provides a very diffused effect that's ideal for flattering portraits. The larger the softbox, the softer the light it produces. The majority are square, but some are rectangular and thin (also called strip lights).

Beauty dish
Beauty dishes are often used, as you may expect, for close-up 'beauty' and make-up shots. They give off a very harsh light in the centre, which enhances make-up, but also highlights flaws on a subject's skin.

Spill (spill kill)
Often supplied with the flash head, they help direct light in a concentrated beam. With portraits, they're useful for lighting backgrounds, but quite harsh when aimed at a subject's face.

Snoot
This conical attachment provides a hard-edge and a directional beam of light that's better suited for backlighting or as a hairlight than providing the key lighting for portraits.

Honeycomb grid
These provide a soft-edged circle of light and are a popular alternative to a snoot. They act in a similar way to a spotlight, but provide a wider angle spot effect. Honeycombs are available with various sizes of grids.

How to set studioflash exposures

If you want to use studioflash, you'll need to set your camera to manual mode. Paul Ward explains the key factors to note to ensure you get set up correctly

Paul Ward FOR SOME PHOTOGRAPHERS, the first time they need to switch their camera to manual mode is when they want to use studioflash. That's because, other than the sync, which triggers the flash, there's no information passing between the camera body and studioflash. It's down to you to set an ISO rating (usually a low 100 or 200), adjust the power of the studioflash, and set an aperture that gives a suitable exposure. The traditional (and best) way to match the studioflash output with the exposure is using a light meter that measures flash. However, rightly or wrongly, digital photographers are increasingly doing away with the separate light meter and instead using the LCD monitor preview facility to work out the best settings via trial and error.

Both methods have their good and bad points so either technique can be used. Here, we explain what they are and show you how to use these techniques for great studioflash photography.

Get connected!

Your camera needs to be connected in some way to the studioflash heads before they can communicate and be told when to fire. There are a number of ways to achieve this and there is a solution to suit all budgets. The cheapest and simplest way to link a camera and flash is with a sync cord. Costing around £10, the lead plugs in to the camera's PC socket at one end and the flash at the other and is very reliable. However, the main drawback is that the photographer is tethered to the studioflash head, so mobility is limited.

A more flexible method is to use an infrared system. A trigger is placed on the camera's hotshoe, while a receiver plugs into the flashhead's sync cord socket. No wires mean the photographer can wander freely around the studio, but infrared systems can be unreliable if the trigger and receiver are not in sight of each other. They are more expensive than a sync lead, but models from brands like of Hama and Hahnel start at around £50.

For the ultimate in flexibility and reliability, most professional photographers opt for a wireless radio triggering system. Like infrared, the radio systems have a trigger and a receiver, but unlike the infrared

versions they don't suffer from line of sight issues as they're triggered by a radio signal. This convenience costs more, with top brands like PocketWizard costing a small fortune. However, third-party brands like Hama, Sekonic, Seculine and Hahnel offer more affordable options – the Hahnel Combi TF costs just £60 and should meet the requirements of most enthusiast photographers.

Histograms

In other photography genres, the histogram can prove a useful tool in the search for a balanced exposure. When it comes to studio photography, Paul suggests it's better to avoid always relying on the histogram: "If you're shooting in a white studio, you're going to get big peaks on your histogram that will look odd, especially if you're used to interpreting a histogram of a landscape image. I think it's much better to judge the exposure on your LCD screen, or if you're shooting tethered, on your laptop." So, if you choose to use the histogram, be wary of overexposed peaks.

Contacts
Hahnel: www.hahnel.ie
Hama: www.hama.co.uk
Seculine: www.intro2020.com
Sekonic: www.sekonic.co.uk

Studioflash: Why manual?

There is a good reason why we use manual mode when using studioflash. If you connect your camera to your studioflash heads with the DSLR set to shutter-priority (Tv) mode, the camera will try to select a (far too large) aperture for you, resulting in a horrendously overexposed image with blown-out highlights. Similarly, if you select aperture-priority (Av) mode then you're likely to be rewarded with a blurry image as the camera automatically sets a long shutter speed based on the ambient light level. Only in manual mode can you control both settings to achieve a balanced exposure using flash.

Know your flash sync speed!

It's important to know your camera's flash sync speed (X-sync), because if you exceed it, you will be blighted by a black bar covering a portion of the image. This black bar is actually the camera's moving shutter curtain preventing the light reaching the whole frame. Conversely, you can select a shutter speed that is slower than the maximum shutter speed without negative effects. Paul tends to keep his camera set a 1/125sec. Here are the typical shutter speeds for big brand digital SLRs:
Canon: 1/200sec; **Nikon:** 1/250sec;
Sony: 1/250sec; **Pentax:** 1/180sec;
Olympus: 1/250sec.

Top techniques for metering studioflash

There are a number of ways you can make sure you get the exposure you want when using studioflash. Some take longer than others, some need a lightmeter, others not. Here are three to get you started...

Technique One: Trial and error

The benefits of this method are that you don't need to buy a lightmeter, saving you money, and because you see the image on the LCD monitor immediately after firing the shutter, it's a very fast technique. If the image is overexposed, you need to lower the ISO and/or select a smaller aperture. If it's underexposed, you'll need to select a wider aperture and/or raise the ISO rating. You can also use the histogram to fine-tune the exposure. The main drawback of this technique is it's not as accurate as using a light meter and you're relying on the quality of the LCD monitor for accuracy. However, so long as you know how to read a histogram you'll get a good exposure. But when using two or more studioflash heads, you're not getting the benefits of metering each light separately.
1) I position my lights depending on the look I want to achieve. I then take an educated guess at the exposure settings – in this case 1/125sec at f/20 (ISO 160) – and take a test shot.
2) My camera's LCD screen allows me to review the image, which reveals it's underexposed and I need to open up the aperture.
3) I change my aperture to f/5.6, but it overexposes the image. You can see that highlights on the skin are what we call 'blown out'.
4) Finally, I change my settings to an aperture between the first two (f/11) and get a balanced exposure that is neither under or overexposed.

Technique two: Take a reading with all lights on

Most amateur photographers – and many pros in fact – use this method to determine studioflash exposures. By taking a single exposure reading with the meter pointing away from the subject and towards the camera, you can quickly take a single meter reading that should give a correct exposure. It's a method that works really well, as you can view the result, then adjust the various power settings on each studioflash head, take another meter reading and set this new exposure setting. It's a less involved method but judging the lighting balance isn't as straightforward – it can also be difficult to judge how each light individually illuminates the subject. Paul shows us how it's done...

1) I make sure the camera is in manual mode and set my ISO (160) into the lightmeter so it can calculate an accurate reading.
2) I take a reading from Kate's face. The meter tells me I need an aperture of f/11 to get the correct exposure so that's exactly what I do.
3) With the subject exposure taken care of by the lightmeter, all I have to do to make the background darker or lighter is to adjust the power setting on the studioflash pointed towards the background.
4) After balancing the background exposure by adjusting the power settings, I'm able to achieve a correctly exposed image of my model, Kate. After some cleaning up in post-production, the image is complete.

Technique Three: Individual light readings

This is the method used by pros looking to get the best possible lighting effect. It involves using a light meter to take an individual exposure reading from each studioflash for very precise control of how each light falls on the subject to give the best possible effect. It's the most involved technique, so takes a little more time and effort, but if you want to master the craft of studioflash lighting, it's one you should keep practising at as it's the method used by most professionals.
1) With my lights set up and turned on, I'm ready to go. Note that I have put a diffuser in place to bounce light back into Kate's face.
2) Input the ISO you're using into the lightmeter and make sure it's in flash mode – usually indicated with a little lightning symbol. By doing this, the light meter will wait until the studioflashes have been fired before telling you what aperture to set on your DSLR.
3) I then take a meter reading from my model's face so I know what aperture will correctly expose the skin. In this case, it's f/11.
4) I take a reading next to the background, which suggests I set f/16. This smaller aperture tells me that, using f/11, the background will be bright, and help me create a high-key effect with the backdrop.
5) By taking multiple readings, I'm able to control both the foreground and background exposures, resulting in a perfectly exposed final image.

Studio set-up: one light

Start learning studio lighting by mastering a series of techniques using simple one-light set-ups

IF YOU WANT TO LEARN how to control your lighting, you're best off starting with just one light. One light is more than sufficient to produce some stunning results and many great photographers still use a single head for their work. After all, outdoors we only have a single light source – the sun. This set-up is very easy to control and the smallest adjustment to the light on your subject has a clear effect. This forces you to fine-tune the light's angle and method of diffusion. And while you'll only have one source of illumination, you can also use reflectors in your set-up to bounce light and fill in any shadows.

The set of images below shows what happens when you position your single light at different heights and angles – as you can see, it's crucial that you learn the do's and don'ts of how to set up your single studioflash head to avoid some of the unflattering results shown below.

As mentioned earlier, you need to set your camera to manual mode and set it to its flash sync speed (if you don't know it, use 1/125sec as a safe bet or refer to the user's manual). The aperture is determined by the meter reading you take, which is easy to do with a one-light set-up. With the sync lead from the light attached, hold the meter in front of the subject's face and press the button to fire the flash and take a reading. By adjusting the power setting on the flash head, you can effectively change the aperture you work with, too. Add power to set a smaller aperture and reduce power to use a wider aperture.

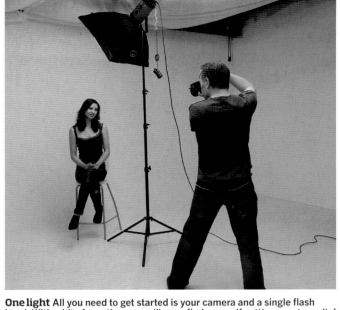

One light All you need to get started is your camera and a single flash head. With a bit of practice, you will soon find yourself getting great results!

1) Lit from above

With the light positioned high above the model's head the light looks natural but creates deep shadows under the eyes, nose and chin. For the best results, get the model to look towards the light. You could also ask her to hold a reflector on her lap to fill in the shadows.

2) Lit from below

Placing the light lower than the model's head, pointing upwards, eradicates any unsightly shadows under the nose and chin. For best results, get the model to look down towards the light, which, as you can see, also makes catchlights appear in the subject's eyes.

3) Lit from the side

Place the light to either the left or right side of your model's face for a strong, directional light, which will keep half of the face in shadow. To increase your chances of capturing catchlights in eyes, it is important to make sure the light is far enough forward.

4) One light & reflector

By holding a reflector close to the face, on the opposite side from the light, you will be able to reduce harsh shadows, much like using a second head. The closer you place it to the model, the stronger the reflection will be (though it helps to have an assistant!).

✓ Tilt the head

When shooting portraits, especially of females, try asking them to tilt their head slightly. This adds an air of friendliness to the shot, making the image look far more relaxed

5) Classic one-light set-up

This technique involves placing the light slightly above and to one side of the model – pointing at a 45° angle to one side and down at 45°. The resulting lighting looks natural and provides well-placed catchlight as well, for a really pleasing, flattering result.

Q&A: Studioflash

How much should I spend on a studioflash system?

We'd recommend you start with a two-head system, with a softbox and umbrella. Tests by *Digital SLR Photography* found several to be excellent, including the Interfit EX150 MkII and the Elinchrom D-Lite 4 IT Studio 2 Go outfit.

What advantages do more expensive outfits offer?

General build quality (and reliability) will be better, but the key benefits are power, features and performance. More power is useful as you can set the lights up further away from your subject, while relative light loss from attachments like softboxes is reduced. You'll find that more expensive heads allow more control over flash output and faster flash recycling times.

Are attachments from different systems compatible?

In general, different brands have their own fittings so aren't compatible. However, Chimera makes speedrings for its softboxes that are compatible with just about any system. Visit: www.chimeralighting.com

How should I set up my camera to use studioflash?

You will need to set it to manual mode, as the metering system will not work with studioflash. Set the shutter speed to the flash sync speed and aperture to the flash meter reading.

How do I take an exposure reading with studioflash?

Use a flash meter connected to a light via a sync lead. Once you've set up the lights, hold the meter in front of the subject's face, take a reading and set the meter's recommended aperture on the camera. Don't forget that the flash meter and camera both need to be set to the same ISO rating!

How do I connect my camera to my studioflash system?

The plug at the end of the studioflash sync lead connects to your camera's PC socket. If your camera hasn't got a socket, buy an adaptor (around £10) that slots on your camera's hotshoe and connect the lead to this. A more expensive option is a wireless trigger that sits on your hotshoe and triggers a receiver on the flash head.

Studio set-up: Two lights

When you feel ready, extend your creative options by introducing a second studio flashhead into the mix

MANY KITS COME WITH two heads, so once you've mastered lighting subjects with a single light, experiment with a second. Often when shooting with a single light, a reflector is used to fill shadows and provide even lighting, but, without an assistant, they can be difficult to position. A second head can be used instead, with the benefit that you can control the power output and add attachments to diffuse or precisely focus the light. The second light is usually called the 'slave' and is triggered when it detects the flash from the primary flash head. Using two lights gives you more scope for different scenarios: you can light the model from different angles, or aim one light at the model and the other at the background.

So how do you meter for two lights? The simplest way is to set up the lights how you would like them, then take a meter reading from the subject's face and take a test shot at the recommended aperture. Consider moving the lights' position, adjusting the light ratio between the two or changing the power. Whatever you decide, take another reading to see what aperture you need and fire another test shot. A more accurate way of taking a reading is to check the exposure of each light in turn (ie only one light on at a time) and adjust accordingly. This will allow you to control the balance of flash between the two lights more accurately, but is a more involved process, so we recommend using the simplest method first and try the second method once you have a bit of experience.

Two lights: This is a typical two-light set-up. The lights are fitted with a softbox and an umbrella to produce a diffused flattering light.

1) Lit from above & below

This is a typical headshot set-up, with the key light at 45° to the subject to give the most flattering light. The second light fills the shadows under the chin. This technique works for almost any subject. Set the key light two stops brighter than the second light.

2) Lit from above & rim light

The key light is above and to the left of the model. The slave light is positioned behind the model, opposite the key light. This throws light over her shoulder, adding a touch of light to her cheek. It adds interest to the shot, and gives her face more of a three-dimensional feel.

3) Lit from back & front

Here, we have one light in front of the model to light her face, and another behind her to light her hair, adding a bit of shine to it. This works well if your model has silky or colourful hair, and is a technique commonly used for 'hair' shots used in magazine advertisements.

4) Butterfly lighting

This is an old-fashioned technique that is not used very much in contemporary photography. By placing both lights above the model, pointing down at a sharp angle, to cast the shadows on her face, you create an interesting 'butterfly' shape under the model's nose.

✅ **Brollies & softboxes**
Brollies are included with most kits as a low-cost diffuser. They do a decent enough job, but it's worth investing in a softbox as soon as possible as they deliver very flattering light for portraits

5) Lit from both sides

Positioning both lights in front of the model, yet off to the sides, is probably the most important two-light technique to learn. It helps to get rid of shadows and gives a very even light across the face. It's useful for eliminating wrinkles, so is commonly used for beauty and make-up shoots. This lighting technique works with just about any subject, and is seen as a 'safe bet' for studio portraiture.

Studio set-up: High-key lighting

High-key lighting is one of the most popular techniques used by contemporary portrait photographers, and it's surprisingly easy

FOR A NUMBER OF YEARS, commercial portrait studios have been making a fortune out of their 'modern-lifestyle' portraits, often taken with wide-angle lenses and almost always shot against a white background. For the technique to work, the lights need to be turned up so high that any skin blemishes become bleached out. The term high-key, although meaning different things to different photographers, generally refers to images with a very low contrast ratio so that there's little difference between the areas of shadow and highlight. The results look fresh and clean, and with a bit of experimentation, it is easy to achieve good results. The shadows you can see are so subtle that the skin often looks flawless without the need for much, if any, post-processing. You will probably find that a lot of modelling agencies use this type of technique for their models' headshots, as it's flattering and hides a multitude of blemishes and imperfections.

Contrary to what many beginners to studio lighting believe, this is a very simple technique to set up, and could even be achieved using only window light and a single reflector. While a reflector and a single studioflash can also work, for the best results you should use at least two studio lights. In this part of the guide, we're going to show you how to create a high-key lighting effect for your portraits using a two-light and a four-light set-up using your budget studioflash outfit.

1) The four-light set-up

You need to point two diffused lights at the subject and aim two lights, with no attachments fitted, at the background. The principle is simple: your subject needs to be correctly exposed, whereas the background should be so grossly overexposed that it's rendered as pure white.

To do this, with the background lights off, set up the two main lights so that they illuminate your subject and work out the correct exposure. Then switch on the background lights and ensure the power setting for them is two stops brighter or more than it is for the subject's lighting. Just remember to take care that the background light isn't so bright that it spills off the backdrop and creates flare that spoils the overall result.

2) The two-light set-up

For this you will need two lights and the corner of a room with white walls and a white ceiling. The first light will be behind you, angled upwards to light the back wall and the ceiling, while the second light is used to illuminate the model's face and add light to the foreground.

The idea here is to light the back wall so that it is overexposed. The light should then bounce off it, so it mimics the effect of a huge softbox. The other flash head, on the opposite side, lights the subject's face (though a reflector can be used instead to bounce light back onto the subject). For most high-key shots of this type, the background lights are around two or three stops brighter than the foreground light. An easy way to do this is to set up the backlight first, taking a shot to ensure it's overexposed. Then put your subject in position and take another shot to see how well-exposed their face is, adjusting the foreground light until the exposure is correct. One thing you might want to try is setting the studioflash on a low power. This will allow you to use a wider aperture for your shots, which result in soft-looking portraits.

✅ Diffusion dilemma

For a high-key effect, you'll need to diffuse your lights as much as possible. To do this, you could use big softboxes or simply bounce the light off a white wall, which will have a similar effect

Create a graphic studio portrait

There's a secret to studio silhouettes – Caroline Wilkinson reveals all here…

Caroline Wilkinson THE SIMPLE LINES and shapes of a silhouette are what makes them so appealing, but as simple as the images are and the technique may seem, getting a decent result is trickier than you might think. Aside from the lighting and exposure, as you're stripping the subject of character and features, the geometry of the pose and outline it creates has to be spot on to create any visual interest. Profile poses are a good place to start as they can accentuate curves, but also look for ways to stop your subject looking too static, such as adding movement and using dynamic shapes or graphic props. Finally, ask your subject to wear black clothing. And remember, if you don't have a studio, you can apply the same principles by shooting against a large window in direct sunlight.

Set-up Place two studioflash heads, set to a mid-power, pointing in either side of a Lastolite HiLite, and have the subject stand in front of the background. Simple. While a Lastolite HiLite is the ideal tool for the job, you can create a similar effect by placing two studio lights, set to full-power, behind and directed at a white paper or fabric backdrop. To avoid the light spilling on to the subject standing in front of the background, attach spills to the studioflash heads to contain the light and try to block any space around the background.

Pick the right power

The strength of the studioflash heads greatly influences the silhouette: too high and you'll get glare that illuminates the subject; too low and the background will be too dark.

Settings & technique

Set your camera to manual mode, its lowest ISO rating, Auto White Balance and image quality to Raw+JPEG. You'll need to dial in your camera's flash sync speed (in my case, that's 1/250sec). Set an aperture of f/11 or f/13 for optimum sharpness. Ask your subject to stand a couple of feet in front of the backdrop for a test shot. If they're illuminated, try turning the studioflash's power down or if the background is too dull, turn it up. Focusing can be a problem in low light, so place the autofocus point over an area of contrast, such as the edge of the body. Or, focus on the subject and switch from AF to manual to stop it hunting between shots. If your subject moves closer or further away from the camera, you may need to refocus.

1 Improve the contrast Even if your exposure is spot on, the background may look dull. Open the image in Adobe Camera Raw and push the *Brightness* and *Contrast* sliders between +80 and +100, with a small tweak to the Clarity for sharpness. Then, in Photoshop, improve the result by adjusting the contrast via *Layer>New Adjustment Layer>Levels*. Finally, crop and convert the image to black & white (*Layer> New Adjustment Layer>Black & White…*).

2 Extend the background If you used a Lastolite HiLite, you may find that you need to extend the background a little. In Photoshop, duplicate the image by dragging the layer down to the *Create a new layer* icon at the bottom of the Layers palette. Select the *Brush Tool* and hold down *alt* to change the cursor into an eyedropper: click on an area of white to take a colour sample, release *alt*, and 'paint' over the areas where the background's not in the frame.

Be inspired! Have fun with different poses: here's a few suggestions to get you started…

Add movement If your subject has long hair, consider introducing a fan to add movement to the image. It immediately stops the shot from looking too static.

Strike a pose Use repeated patterns and shapes to add interest. Try to contain the viewer's eye within the frame and subject by connecting lines.

Jump Ask the subject to leap or jump for an energetic image: keep an eye on the pose to make sure that there's space around the limbs for a defined outline.

Be abstract Concentrate on the composition and zoom in on the curved lines of the body or details like the feet for less conventional but alluring images.

Final image
Introducing props, like this
umbrella, can add extra visual
interest to a picture. Experiment
to see what effects you can get by
adding semi-transparent fabric
and/or a fan to your set-up, too.
This image was taken using
1/250sec at f/13 (ISO 200).

Master the secrets of classic film noir lighting

Hollywood has given us many classics, not least its iconic lighting technique: a glamorous, low-key style that all portrait photographers can master using our expert advice

Bjorn Thomassen
WHEN PHOTOGRAPHERS THINK of the 'Golden Age' of Hollywood, most recollect the likes of Rita Hayworth, Elizabeth Taylor and Vivien Leigh, not as on-screen sirens, but as iconic subjects of dramatic Hollywood portraits. The classic Hollywood portrait of the 1940s in particular was typified by its high contrast black & white images, created using strong directional light, with strategically placed shadows to add depth and drama. Today, Hollywood lighting is considered an art form that many still love to recreate – including us. While its style might be seen as dated, it's an immensely useful technique to learn.

Compared to the portraits we shoot today, posing is quite rigid and, as it's not the most flattering style of lighting, it's best suited to people with good skin. The slightest imperfection will be amplified. Being able to control and focus the light is key, as you need to be very targeted with where the light falls. Here, I've used a studioflash with a medium reflector dish and barndoors attached to direct the light, but taping thick black card to all four sides of your flash can work just as well. The hard light from the studioflash is then tempered by the light bouncing off the reflector on the opposite side, before reaching the model. A second light is also used on the opposite side to accent the edges of the subject.

While most Hollywood portraits are against a plain black background, some images show texture in their backdrop, which is why we've chosen to use a carefully hung white background to show you how to create this effect should you want to use it. One of the reasons we're using barndoors, too, is to stop the spill of light on to the background, as without it the white backdrop will turn black, but still retain some tonal detail.

Original

Camera settings

(M) **Metering & exposure:** The aperture you use depends on how much background detail you want in focus, how close the subject is to the backdrop and on the power of your lights. Here, the model is about a metre away, so f/5.6 provides enough depth-of-field to render her in focus but blur the backdrop. Hold the light meter by the face, but pointing towards the light source – not the camera – so it can accurately measure the amount of light falling on the subject. Now adjust the power of the studioflash until you get the aperture you want. With the camera in manual mode and the flash sync speed set, dial in your appropriate aperture and take your shot.

Lighting set-up

Place the main light close to the subject to have better control over the fall-off of the light: you want to avoid it illuminating the subject's lap. Position the main light 90° to the camera, pointing down 45° on the subject. Place the model in a ¾ pose, so that the side of the face receiving the most light is turned away from the camera. By doing this, it casts a triangular shadow on the cheek closest to the camera, which is characteristic of the lighting style. The plane of the face needs to be relative to the main light for the shadow to be cast correctly. Every set-up is different, but when positioning the reflector to soften the main light and act as a fill-in, remember the law of reflection and avoid placing it too close to the model, as it may counteract the striking modelling and shadows you've created. Mine is placed approximately four feet away from the model. To add more dimensionality to the image, an accent light has been added three feet away from the subject and angled upwards at 30°, so light falls on to the opposite edges of the model. The set-up works on a lighting ratio of 3:1, as the accent light shouldn't overpower the main light.

Studioflash

Wireless trigger

Barndoors

Reflector dish

Reflector

Final image
Shot at 1/160sec at f/5.6, this Hollywood portrait looks even more striking with a soft sepia tone. After some skin retouching using the Healing Brush Tool and small tonal adjustments using Levels, add a duotone effect by going to *Image>Grayscale* then *Image>Duotone*, then choose Sepia style from the *Preset* menu.

SIMPLE STEPS TO BETTER PICTURES

FAMILY PORTRAITS

IDEAS & INSPIRATION TO HELP YOU TAKE FAMILY PICTURES YOU'LL TREASURE FOREVER

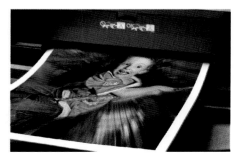

The basic principles to photographing kids

Every child is unique and each has to be handled in their own special way. But there are certain steps to follow that can help you take your best ever pictures

IT ISN'T ALWAYS EASY, but capturing great shots of kids is one of the most rewarding moments in photography. Because they're often a law unto themselves, children can be a real challenge to photograph. However, by learning a few basic skills and knowing how to make the most of their exuberant nature, you should be able to build up a nice collection of images. Strangely enough, when shooting kids, one of the key factors for success isn't anything to do with photography, it's actually all to do with how well you interact with the subject. It's essential that your subject feels comfortable and relaxed having their picture taken by you, otherwise they just won't look natural in the shots. Ideally, for at least the first ten minutes, keep any camera gear out of sight and spend the time chatting to the child and the parents. Only once they've got used to you should you think about getting out your camera and taking pictures. You'll normally find that younger children are generally the easiest to get on with and teenagers can be the most difficult, as they're more self-conscious and so often more reluctant to have their picture taken.

What sort of pictures should you aim to take?

Well, that's something that you, the parents and (in the case of shooting older children), the subjects themselves can decide. In the past, portraits were very formal, but, actually, the most pleasing portraits are those that capture relaxed subjects with happy and natural expressions. Shooting in the sitter's home is usually a good starting point. They'll feel comfortable in their surroundings and you'll have a multitude of different outfits and props if you require them. One more thing on clothing – don't get the children to wear their Sunday best as they won't feel comfortable, but instead have them dress in casual clothes or a favourite outfit.

As good as the home is, though, there is much to be said about heading out and shooting on location. Virtually anywhere is suitable – local parks, open countryside, industrial areas, beaches and city centres each have different attractions and moods that can add to a portrait. And remember: there are countless ways to compose the subject in the frame; from head shots to full-length body shots and images where they're relatively small in the frame. The options are endless, so use your imagination.

Vary your composition Two ways to dramatically alter your portraits: ask your subject to adopt different poses and try different crops; ie face close-ups, head-and-shoulder shots or full-length body shots.

How should you set up your digital camera?

When shooting portraits of kids, you'll need to be able to think on your feet and work fast, as while there will be moments where they're posing nicely, most of the time you'll be trying to keep up with their antics. Here's our recommended settings

1) Exposure mode: The best bet is to use aperture-priority mode. We'd suggest you start off by setting f/5.6 and, to be honest, you can more or less leave it set to f/5.6 for the entire time. At this setting, you're working with a shallow depth-of-field that ensures your subject's face is sharp, but the background is thrown out of focus. What you'll need to keep your eye on is the shutter speed as you want to ensure it's fast enough to avoid shake. Increase the ISO rating (to a maximum of ISO 800-1000) when the shutter speed drops too low. Try to keep it at 1/200sec or faster and you should be fine if you're using a 50-200mm, or 1/300sec if it's a 70-300mm that you're using.

2) Autofocus: You can leave your camera set to multi-point AF mode if you want, but you run the risk of focusing on a shoulder, forehead, tip of the nose etc and not on the eyes, which is what you want to ensure is pin-sharp. We'd suggest you set your AF to single-point AF and use the central focusing sensor, which offers the best sensitivity. Set your AF mode to S (S-AF, AF-S) so that when you focus on the eye, you can lock the focus by pressing the shutter button halfway down, then recompose and take the shot.

3) Metering: Stick to multi-zone metering and you shouldn't have any problems. If your subject is predominantly dark, take one shot and check the LCD monitor; if detail is missing, add +1EV using the exposure compensation facility.

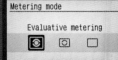

4) File format: Shoot in Raw for the maximum control over image quality and colour balance. However, when shooting fast sequences, it can slow your shooting rate because the buffer has to handle more data. Shoot JPEG only if you're not confident about converting Raw to JPEG or when memory space on your card is limited.

5) White Balance: Ideally, set White Balance to suit the lighting conditions. If you're unsure what to use, set your camera to Auto White Balance (AWB). Bear in mind, though, if you're shooting in Raw, you can easily change settings once you have the images on your computer.

Final image
The adorable nature of children means that you don't have to try to be too clever when taking their portrait. Make sure the lighting's good and the child is relaxed and you're almost there!

Keep it simple!
You'll see this tip emerge again and again, but the secret to great portraits is to try to keep everything as simple as possible, from your gear to the lighting

BRETT HARKNESS

Photographing the kids: Be prepared

You can improve your chances of success by being ready in advance!

What kit should you use? Your choice of kit will largely be influenced by the type of pictures you're taking and your location. If you're looking to shoot natural portraits and working with natural light, it's best to keep your kit to a minimum – a DSLR or CSC fitted with a zoom, along with a reflector, is often all you need. Sometimes you'll want extra lighting and while your camera's integral flash can provide fill-in, a hotshoe-mounted flashgun with bounce facility is better, while a basic studioflash set-up offers scope for creative lighting. However, the more artificial lighting you add, the more effort you'll need to put in to make sure shots look natural.

Using natural light: From a beginner's perspective, working with natural light is a far easier proposition than having to use studioflash. But while there are not any power settings to twiddle with, there are still a number of factors that have to be considered when working with ambient light. For instance, the nature of daylight varies according to the weather conditions and time of day. On a sunny day, light is harsh and unflattering, on very overcast days, it is dull, while shooting in the shade can give cool, flat results. By knowing how to control lighting conditions using reflectors, diffusers or flash, you can manipulate the light to produce high-quality portraits. A reflector is an indispensable accessory for virtually every form of lighting, while a diffuser is ideal for strong sunlight (see panel below).

Using studioflash: While daylight makes a fantastic source of portrait lighting, it's not always available when and where you need it. Being able to use studioflash offers you the chance to shoot when the weather's poor, at night or when you're indoors. Using one or two flash heads with a brolly or softbox and a reflector can give you great results with minimal effort once you've established how to position the lights and how to adjust the power of the flash heads. In the past, studioflash kits were usually only available to the wealthier amateurs and professionals, but there are now a number of affordable kits available. And because you're able to instantly review your images on the LCD monitor, it's far easier to check lighting set-ups and make adjustments than ever before. If you decide that you would like to try out studioflash, then check out the studioflash sections of this guide for expert advice on the best studioflash kits, accessories and techniques.

Natural light

DANIEL LEZANO

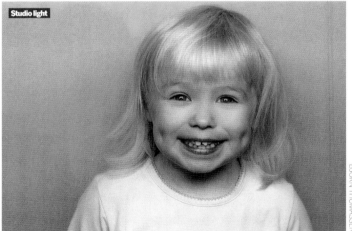
Studio light

BJORN THOMASSEN

Ideas for outdoor locations

Stuck for ideas on where to photograph great images of the kids? To be honest, almost any location is suitable, but here's a selection of tried-and-tested backdrops…

Industrial area: Large corrugated doors, graffiti and warehouses with broken windows and skips are all locations that have distinctive character. It may sound strange to some, but we reckon it's the perfect place to shoot some great portraits of the kids.

Farm: If you can visit a local farm and you're able to wander safely around it, you'll find that the barns, farmhouses, bales and general scenery can make for really interesting pictures.

Pillars or columns: You'll find the pillars and columns outside some museums, cathedrals and large libraries make great backgrounds. If you've more than one child in the scene, have them poke their heads around different pillars.

Weather-beaten doors: The texture of old wooden doors makes an ideal portrait backdrop. As well as brown, splintery wood, look for painted doors where the paint is old and flaky.

The local park: Feeding ducks; sat on a bench munching sandwiches or enjoying an ice cream; sat beneath a tree shaded from the sun… The picture-taking possibilities are endless!

Lighting accessories

Ideal accessories to help you control and manipulate light are as follows:

Reflectors: A hand/held reflector is a must. Ideally, go for one with a white side and a silver side. White reflects less light than silver, but its effect is more subtle and natural. Silver is more efficient but should be used with care as its effect can be overpowering. Gold has a similar efficiency to silver but gives a warm glow, making it a good choice if your subject is a little pale or you're shooting in shade or on a cool winter's day.

Diffusers: Worth considering if you plan to shoot in direct sunlight. Place a diffuser between the sun and subject to bathe your subject in a soft, diffused light that is ideal for flattering portraits. Diffusers are available in different sizes and diffusing 'strengths'. Some can be supported on stands, but the majority are hand-held, although you'll need a friend to assist as they're easily blown around in the wind.

Clothing

What your subject wears is important as it needs to fit with the general mood of the image. Ask the pros their opinion on what children should wear and you'll get a variety of answers ranging from 'plain is best' to 'can't beat colours' and 'stripes are super'. Some base their choice on location or time of year. In other words, what's best is very subjective! However, what they all say is that your subject should feel very comfortable with what they're wearing and that for the majority of the time, casual clothing works best. So for boys, a pair of jeans and a T-shirt or fleece is good, while for girls, jeans and a blouse/T-shirt and cardigan is fine. Have them bring along a small selection of tops so that you get them to change outfits during the shoot. You should also give some thought to jewellery and props like hats and sunglasses.

Let's talk babies...

A new family member is one of the main reasons people buy a digital camera. Here's how to guarantee great baby shots

FEW THINGS HAVE AS MUCH OF AN 'aah' factor for cuteness as a baby. Those chubby cheeks, big eyes and toothless smiles are the perfect ingredients for wonderful portraits. However, as photogenic as babies are, they're not the easiest of subjects to shoot. For one, they're not going to pay any attention to what you're saying, so forget asking them to look out of the window or smile. Instead, expect lots of dribbling, snoozing, crying and looking everywhere except at the camera. Another obstacle you'll need to overcome, especially with babies just a few months old, is that they'll still not be strong enough to support themselves, so you'll have to shoot them lying down or being supported. For that reason, many parents and family members are left frustrated that they can't capture the latest addition to the family as well as they'd like to. It's no surprise when you consider many get too close with a wide-angle lens and pop up the integral flash. The result is a distorted baby grimacing after the nth flash burst of its short life.

So, you've got a hard task ahead of you, but there are several things in your favour. The first is that your subject isn't very mobile, so isn't going to run off anywhere. And because one or both parents will be present, they'll generally be comfortable and happy – especially if you plan to shoot after one of their regular naps or feeds.

Before taking any pictures, spend a few minutes talking to the baby, waving toys around, letting them hold your finger; anything that puts them at ease. Smile a lot and don't feel daft for making silly noises or talking in a cutesy voice; it all works at establishing an initial bond.

If you're shooting indoors, place your subject near patio/french doors; if outdoors, look for an area of well-lit shade. You'll want to work fast and be able to hand-hold the camera, so set a high ISO (400-800) and use a wide aperture. Look to shoot against as plain a background as possible; try shooting against light and dark backdrops, reviewing your monitor to see which is most suitable.

A baby's eyes are relatively large in relation to the rest of their face, so ensure at least one is sharply in focus. Change your viewpoint, shooting from above and then lying down to shoot from the baby's eye level or lower.

Once you start taking pictures, you'll need to work fast. If you want, set the frame rate to continuous and shoot sequences whenever your subject is looking directly at you. Most of the images won't be worth keeping, but with any luck you'll get a handful of shots that the parents will love. The better alternative is to leave the drive to single-frame advance and opt for fewer pictures taken with a little more craft and purpose.

TOP: Young babies are often too weak to support themselves, so use furniture as an aid and, if possible, have a parent or assistant close by to prevent any accidents!

ABOVE: Be bold and try unusual compositions. Babies usually have very large eyes and so close crops and a very shallow depth-of-field allow you to emphasise this.

Top tips: Babies

1) Grab their attention You can usually get them to look at you if you hold a toy and give it a shake or a squeeze just before you plan to fire the shutter.

2) Don't overdo it! A ten-minute session is long enough. Take a tea break, then try again!

3) Keep your cool You should not get frustrated or annoyed if the shoot's not going to plan. Accept that there's always the chance that you won't get any, let alone many, suitable pictures.

4) Expect mess! Keep a kitchen roll handy for wiping away any baby sick and some tissues for dribble or mucus from noses. Babies produce surprisingly large amounts of both!

5) Get creative If the baby's not looking at the camera, try unusual angles and compositions that might make a good shot, or concentrate on shooting hands, feet or other small details.

Hands & feet

You should make sure you take some shots of the baby's hands and feet. This is a good picture to try when the baby is only a few days old as they'll be sleeping most of the time and their wrinkly skin adds to the effect. Use soft light and keep colours pale and neutral, set a wide aperture for shallow depth-of-field and experiment with different angles and viewpoints. Try images in colour and black & white.

ALL IMAGES: BRETT HARKNESS

Baby behaviour
If you're very patient, you may be able to catch a moment when the baby is messing around and looking straight at the camera!

Convert to b&w
Bear in mind that baby pictures are ideal for converting to black & white, so you should always consider turning some of your favourite shots into much-loved monochrome images

Photographing toddlers

The early years are exciting times for parent and child. Get set to capture special moments with your camera

IF YOU HAD TO SUM UP toddlers in one word, it would most likely be 'unpredictable'. From the moment that babies discover the mobility of their own two wrinkly little feet, they're up and about with a mind of their own, exploring their new world. It's something they'll continue to do for a number of years, so you've plenty of time to get some great shots of them in their first years of discovery. That said, kids grow up extremely quickly, too, so you don't want to miss out on never-to-be-repeated moments. You need to be prepared for anything they're likely to do, so if they pull a face, fall over, break into fits of giggles, or anything else that kids of this age often do, you'll have your camera ready to capture every treasured moment.

It's really important that you spend a bit of time getting to know the kids and more importantly, give them a chance to get to know you too. If you're photographing your own kids or your family or friends' children, this isn't such an issue, but if it's a child you don't know, imagine how they'll feel if a complete stranger starts taking their photos. Spend ten to 15 minutes in the company of the parents chatting to the child and gaining their trust, and you'll find they're far more relaxed and responsive.

A telezoom is the best choice of lens, as you can shoot at a distance without your subject even knowing they're being photographed, allowing them to behave completely naturally. If your images aren't as candid as you'd like them to be, spend a little more time playing with your subject so they get more used to you being around. They'll soon lose interest in you, allowing you to shoot more freely. Use a reflector if shooting indoors – you'll find many toddlers see the reflector as a large, fun, shiny toy, so if they're playing with it, aim for tight portraits while their faces are well lit! Don't carry too much kit – it will get in the way and you'll invariably be switching lenses when the best photo opportunities arise.

You need to have a lot of patience when photographing young children. Don't try to manipulate them; if they decide they've had enough, then let them roam for five minutes, and then try and coax them into a few more shots. But always be ready. When the chance comes, your camera should be correctly set for you to capture the moment before it's gone.

ABOVE: Allow toddlers freedom and it won't be long before they forget about the camera, allowing you to capture very natural candids.

LEFT: Always keep in mind that you can create sets of images that tell a story. Triptychs (a set of three images) are very popular and worth trying out.

Make the studio fun!

If you're using studioflash, it's not unusual for toddlers to get a little anxious, so find things that easily distract them. It's natural for parents to bring some toys with them, but you can have some of your own there too as young kids love to try out new toys. Contributor Bjorn Thomassen has another solution: "I've found that bubbles can really work at capturing their attention and they'll usually widen their eyes and smile when bubbles are near. I also have a Disney CD playing quietly in the background as these familiar songs help put them in a 'happy place'."

Gift ideas

Framed photo-story
Producing framed prints that are made up of a multiple of images is a great way to provide a photo-story of the day. You'll find many photo outlets and art stores, as well as some large department stores, sell frames with mounts for holding several images. It makes an interesting and eye-catching variation to the normal method of mounting a single image within a frame.

Top tips: Toddlers

1) Make the shoot fun!
The more the session is about having fun and less about the pictures, the better. You'll get the most from your photo sessions when you take the kids' mind off what's going on.

2) Capture break times
Keep shooting even during the 'downtime' when kids are taking a break, having a drink etc, as you may get great candid shots.

3) Let kids do their thing
Keep giving instructions and they'll soon get bored or upset. Instead, allow them to do their own thing and occasionally see if you can prompt them to pose.

4) Change their clothes
It's amazing how a quick outfit change can give images a whole new look and feel. Add a change of location and you'll come away with a real mix of images.

5) Include the parents!
Don't forget to get Mum and Dad involved – even if they say no!

Timid toddlers
If your subject's shy, play games with them, such as peeking over chair backs or around doors, then grab the shot.

Photographing youngsters

They can be precocious, naughty and downright cheeky. But at this age, kids are often at their most photogenic, too!

IT'S GENERALLY ACCEPTED by many parents that the most enjoyable years of childhood are when their kids are aged between five and ten. These are the years when children develop their personality and a small sense of independence, which can lead to some fantastic photographic opportunities.

These younger years have the potential to deliver the best child portraits. Because the kids can run around on their own, you've scope to capture some excellent candids. Fit a telezoom to your DSLR (a 50-200mm or 70-300mm) and you can keep your distance so your subject carries on oblivious to the camera. After you've taken a few shots, find a good viewpoint, call their name and, with your camera set to continuous drive, rattle off a few frames when they look over.

Kids of this age are (fairly) responsive to instruction, so if you need them to sit, stand, turn around etc, they're more than likely to do so. This allows you to shoot a good mix of pictures, from candids to more staged shots, in a short space of time. And because your subject will start to get a little bored after a few minutes and begin messing about again, you can expect a few silly faces and poses towards the end of the session.

Be relaxed about how you 'pose' your subjects. Ask them to stand/sit by a particular place and take a couple of shots. If they look tense, get them to shake their arms and head to get them to relax and laugh as they do this, so they feel like they're having fun. Take a couple more shots, tell them they're doing great and get them to raise/drop their chin, tilt their head and so on until you get the shot you're after. Try a variety of viewpoints and crops to really mix up the shots. And at the end of the shoot, tell them to go crazy for a couple of minutes and capture them at their least sensible!

As well as head-and-shoulder shots, take full-length body shots; if they have a unique sense of style, use it and show it! They might like to wear hats, bright colours or dress up as Superman. Your ultimate goal should be to take a good mix of images that together captures various aspects of your subject's nature. As always, if you can, have an 'assistant' handy to hold a reflector or diffuser and give you added control of the lighting.

Doorways are ideal for youngsters to pose in front of. Choose clothes that suit the colour of the door and if the youngster's wearing layers of tops, get them to lose the fleece/jumper after a bit and pose in their T-shirt to change it up. Use a reflector for that extra bit of added light.

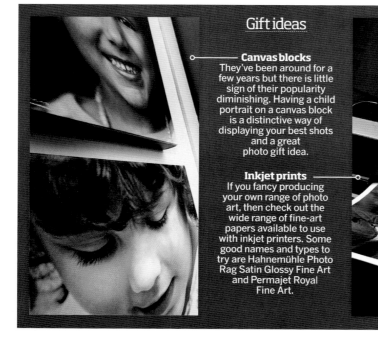

Gift ideas

Canvas blocks
They've been around for a few years but there is little sign of their popularity diminishing. Having a child portrait on a canvas block is a distinctive way of displaying your best shots and a great photo gift idea.

Inkjet prints
If you fancy producing your own range of photo art, then check out the wide range of fine-art papers available to use with inkjet printers. Some good names and types to try are Hahnemühle Photo Rag Satin Glossy Fine Art and Permajet Royal Fine Art.

Top tips: Youngsters

1) Work quickly
A telezoom lens (ie 50-200mm) allows you to quickly change the composition from tight head shots to full-body shots.

2) Ensure they're at ease
Before you start taking pictures, explain what you plan to do and have a laugh with them to help them relax.

3) Be positive! Constantly tell them they're a natural at having their picture taken and that they look really good in the shots. Even at a young age, kids will benefit from this encouragement.

4) Let them play! If they start messing around, let them play and capture some candids, before stopping them to get ready for the next shoot.

5) Reward them! A bribe (toy, sweets etc) always works a treat and a reward for their efforts will help them say 'yes' to having their picture taken again!

Don't forget teddy!
Some youngsters, even those getting close to double figures, can't live without their favourite teddy! Let them include their comfort toy in some shots as it will help them relax in front of the camera.

Time for the teenagers!

Treat teenagers as adults and you're sure to get the best from them

AS EVERY PARENT will testify, kids rapidly develop independence when they reach secondary school. As a photographer, this generally means your subjects need to be treated more like adults than children if you're going to have any chance of getting them to perform in front of the camera. So while you may want to offer some advice on what they should wear, for instance, don't be negative if they turn up wearing the complete opposite of what you asked them to. Work with them and ask them to change outfits when you've shot a few frames to see if they'll go with what you want them to wear.

You'll generally find that they have a short attention span and act as if they have better things to do than have their picture taken. But if you're friendly, interested in what they have to say and listen attentively to ideas on how they want to be shot, it will go a long way to keeping them on your side. If you can get your subjects to enjoy what they're doing, the shoot will be a breeze as they'll naturally shift from pose to pose after every shot!

Kids are at their most self-conscious when they're in their teens and while some are pure exhibitionists, the majority are worried about how they'll look in pictures, especially if their hormones are playing havoc with their skin. Your aim should generally be to capture them in flattering light, make them look like 'grown-ups' rather than kids, and try to get them to enjoy the experience.

Teenagers can be real fun to work with, so try to capture this in your images. Have your assistant or a friend try to make them laugh and be ready to capture the moment. Many teenagers have strong interests so try to incorporate this into the image where possible, either through what they wear or props.

BRETT HARKNESS

What do they want?

As well as a selection of pictures that you and the parents like, you should also make sure to ask the subject how they would like to be shot. You may be surprised at what they come up with. When we asked Katie for ideas on how she'd like to be shot, she said she wanted a nice black & white image looking away from the camera and showed us a picture in a magazine. It wasn't the sort of picture we'd planned, but we spent some time setting it up and capturing the sort of look that Katie wanted. For this image, we sat Katie next to some diffused French doors so that she was side-lit, then set up a studioflash with a small softbox on the floor to provide a little light from low down on the opposite side. The image was then converted to black & white using Photoshop.

Mono lighting
If you plan to convert images to black & white you don't need to worry about colour casts from the lighting. Leave your camera on AWB.

Top tips: Teenagers

1) Make sure they're happy, relaxed and having fun. You'll end up with far better images than if they're bored and uninterested.

2) Ask them if they've any favourite photos from magazines or the internet and see if you can shoot them in a similar style.

3) Give them a rough idea of what you'd like them to wear (ie plain T-shirt, jeans etc), but make sure they're happy with your choice.

4) Try not to sound too formal when talking to them, but be careful not to use words like 'cool' if you think it could backfire!

5) When you've got a good shot, show it to them on the LCD screen. If they like what they see, you'll give them the needed interest to continue.

6) Don't shoot with their parents or friends watching as they'll probably feel embarrassed – ask those who aren't being included to leave the room!

7) Give them a small gift (ie £10 iTunes voucher) as a thank you and send them some prints of the best shots. It's a small price to pay for their time and also means they'll be happy to pose for more pictures in future!

Final image
Teenagers usually enjoy a fashion portrait shoot as it allows them to pose in their favourite clothes. Make sure to produce some prints of their favourite shots as a thank you.

BRETT HARKNESS

Adding fun to your portraits

If teenagers are having plenty of fun, it's not difficult to capture lots of fantastic shots. These great tricks should help…

Daniel Lezano HAYLEY (16) AND KATIE (14) are part of my extended family and I've known them for around ten years. They're no strangers to having their pictures taken by me, often for various features in *Digital SLR Photography* magazine, but this was the first time they'd been asked to pose 'as themselves', rather than to show specific techniques or as part of a camera test. A few days before the session, I asked them how they wanted to be shot – they didn't really have any clear ideas, so I suggested they look through various fashion titles and back issues of *Digital SLR Photography* for ideas. They were drawn to nice black & white portrait shots to 'fashion lifestyle' shoots similar to the type taken by contributors Brett Harkness and Bjorn Thomassen. As for their parents, the request was simple: produce a nice series of images of the two of them together.

I had already scouted out a location full of character in the centre of their home town, Stamford in Lincolnshire, and on the day, the overcast conditions were ideal. A set of large blue doors provided the ideal backdrop for 'fashion portraits'. We began by asking the two sisters to mess around and make the whole photo experience more fun. I snapped away while they pulled faces, pushed each other about and gave each other piggybacks. After a couple of minutes, they realised the shoot had the potential to be lots of fun, so they were lively and responsive to my instructions. I shot the two of them leaning against each other, hugging and so on, and the results were excellent.

Next, I shot Hayley on her own. Running through a few poses and shooting from various angles resulted in several nice shots within minutes. The silver side of the reflector was ideal for bouncing light on to Hayley and filling in unwanted shadows. I asked Katie to hold the reflector to keep her involved and interested. As well as full-body poses, we took some head-and-shoulder shots and tight crops of her face. I tried to let things flow with minimal interruptions, but kept an eye out for small details; asking Hayley to move stray hairs away from her eyes and also removing her pink necklace. We had Katie use the reflector as a makeshift fan for a bit of fun, blowing Hayley's hair in all directions while I fired away. The results were hit and miss, but it kept their enthusiasm high throughout the shoot. With both very relaxed, I took some more of the two of them together, this time with an assistant holding the reflector. In the space of 20 minutes, it was pretty clear that we had captured a real mix of pictures and there were several images from the shoot that could be printed and framed.

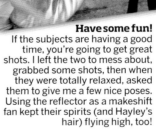

Have some fun!
If the subjects are having a good time, you're going to get great shots. I left the two to mess about, grabbed some shots, then when they were totally relaxed, asked them to give me a few nice poses. Using the reflector as a makeshift fan kept their spirits (and Hayley's hair) flying high, too!

Gift ideas

Floating panels
A modern and stylish way of displaying your favourite images is to have them made into a floating panel to decorate your home. The image is printed and placed on a thin sheet of lightweight aluminium which, when mounted on the wall using its batons (inset), appears to be 'floating'. Try photobox.co.uk for something similar; prices start at £27.99. And websites like bagsoflove.co.uk offer really good value large canvas prints.

Photo books
A number of firms offer photo books made up of your own pictures and text. We made our own using Apple iPhoto software, then paid for it online – a week later, it had arrived in the post!

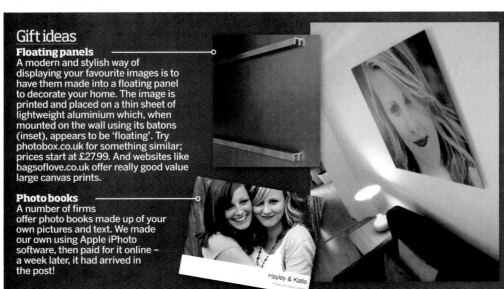

Hayley & Katie

Teen shoot: Summary

✔ Formal settings are nowhere near as much fun as the outdoors for a lifestyle shoot. The latter is also far better for revealing more of the subject's personality.

✔ Having two (or more) teenagers together means they have more fun during the session and this makes for much better pictures. And when each is being shot on their own, the other can be kept involved by assisting with holding the reflector.

✔ Don't believe the stereotype of teenagers as grungy, sulky and introverted. Most are intelligent, streetwise and fun to photograph.

✔ Before the day of the shoot, be sure to mention make-up if you're photographing girls. Make sure they only apply a small amount to cover blemishes and don't go over the top!

Image details
Exposure: 1/400sec at f/4.5 (ISO 250).

SIMPLE
STEPS TO
BETTER
PICTURES

DIGITAL TECHNIQUES

IMPROVE YOUR IMAGES & ADD CREATIVE EFFECTS WITH OUR POST-PROCESSING TUTORIALS

Create a caricature

You don't always have to be reserved with your retouching – have a bit of fun and use the Liquify filter to exaggerate features for comic effect

Caroline Wilkinson SOMETIMES USING THE Liquify filter to create bigger eyes, lips or muscles can flatter a subject, but if taken to the extreme this filter can distort a person beyond recognition. Normally we'd advocate making many small adjustments to avoid this and to ensure natural and subtle results by slowly building up the effect – but where's the fun in that?

For this tutorial, enlarge that Brush Size, increase its Rate and boost that Pressure for some uninhibited fun and to distort a portrait into a caricature. Even though you'll be exaggerating your subject's key features, there should still be an easily identifiable visual likeness, so try to build on what's already there. For instance, if they have big eyes, make them bigger. If they have a large nose, exaggerate it even more. One of the distinguishing features of caricature is the distortion of perspective: making the head much bigger than the body or the forehead a lot wider than their tapered chin, or visa versa, for instance. Have a go with your family photos and why not send us your funniest faces?

Top tip

Reconstruct
If you want to undo your distortions, you can click *Restore All* in the *Reconstruct Options* panel to revert the image back to its original state. However, if you wish to only reconstruct a part of your image, select the *Reconstruct Tool* in the toolbar and click on the area you want to restore. If you do use this tool, make sure the *Reconstruct Mode* (in the Options panel) is set to *Revert* so the image can backstep to its original state.

Original

1 Create a duplicate layer Open the image in Photoshop and go to *Layer>Duplicate Layer*, so you're working on a copy. Now click *Filter>Liquify* to load the layer into the Liquify filter. The dialog opens with a preview image in the centre and the toolbar to the left with the options bar to the right. Zoom in to the picture so it fills the preview window to make adjustments easier.

2 Inflate the eyes A good place to start distorting is the eyes. Select the *Bloat Tool* and a *Brush Size* that's as big as the eye socket. Place the cursor in the centre of the pupil, then click and hold to see the eye inflate. If the effect is too fast or too heavy, reduce the *Brush Rate* or increase it if it's not fast enough. For the best effect, it's important to click in one area, then drag the tool.

3 Bloat the forehead To refine the shape of the eye, reduce the *Brush Size* and click around the edge of the eye to bloat that too. If the pupil changes shape, simply click in the centre again. Use the *Pucker Tool* to reduce the overall effect. While you've got the *Bloat Tool* selected, increase the *Brush Size* so it's proportional with the forehead and click to expand this area.

4 Make a mask Reduce the *Brush Size* again and puff out the cheeks a little with the *Bloat Tool*. To target the teeth, but not the lips, select the *Freeze Mask Tool* and click the *Show Mask* icon in the Options panel. Adjust the *Brush Size* and paint over the areas you don't want to be affected. If you do too much, switch to the *Thaw Mask Tool* and simply erase what you don't need.

5 Enlarge the teeth Now with the *Forward Warp Tool* set to a brush no bigger than the tooth, click and drag the bottom of the tooth down to enlarge it without affecting the lip. When you're done, use the *Thaw Mask Tool* to erase the mask. Now use the *Forward Warp Tool* to subtly extend the smile if you need to or switch to the *Bloat Tool* to puff up the lips, nose and ears.

6 Reshape the face Now use the *Forward Warp Tool* (set to a large brush of 300-600, with a medium *Pressure* of 50 and a *Rate* of 26), to distort the face. To narrow the chin, click on the jaw line and drag it in to narrow the face. To elongate the chin, click and drag downwards. You can also use the same technique to stretch the neck by pushing down the shoulders.

Funny faces!
This is an easy and enjoyable technique to try on your children's photographs or a family portrait. Give it a go!

Add texture to photographs

Mastering the fundamentals of Layers, Layer Masks and Blend Modes create new possibilities for post-production. Find out how to combine all three to apply textures and add impact to your pictures

Caroline Wilkinson ADDING TEXTURE TO a photograph can produce beautifully artistic effects and, while the results may look complicated, it's relative simple to achieve a strong finish. The principle behind it is mastering how to blend layers together by becoming accustomed with the various methods of doing this, as each one produces a different end result.

Textures aren't something that should be used recklessly: it's easy to allow them to overwhelm a perfectly good picture. Your choice of texture should work with the image to enhance its mood, colour and, ultimately, impact. However, picked carefully they can add character to an ordinary snapshot and improve a picture's appeal tenfold.

To truly understand how this technique works, we'd advise you read the latest *Photoshop for Photographers* MagBook, which explains in-depth how Layers, Layer Masks and Blend Modes work together. As an outline, though, when applying a texture, make sure it's on top of the image layer in the Layers palette for it to affect the image. You can then use the Opacity slider at the top of the Layers palette to control the transparency of the texture and/or apply a Blend Mode from the drop-down menu at the top of the Layers palette. In general, we've found that Multiply, Screen, Soft Light and Overlay work the best when merging layers. There are no rules for how many layers you should use, but the more you do apply, the more the original character of the image will be altered.

ISTOCKPHOTO

Original

How to use

Layer Masks
A Layer Mask allows you to hide detail from the layer it's applied to, revealing the image beneath without erasing it. When the Layer Mask is selected, simply add the colour black to the mask to hide image detail and change to the colour white to restore the detail. Use the **X** key to quickly switch between the colours.

Hot Key

Changing Blend Modes
To quickly apply Blend Modes, hold down *Shift* and press + and – keys to move up and down the list, respectively. Or, for an even quicker way, press *Alt/Option, Shift* and the letter for that particular blend mode, eg *O* for Overlay or *S* for Soft Light.

Final image
Choosing textures that enhance the warm colours of the original image complement the image as well as creating a painterly effect.

1 Open your image Duplicate your photograph (*Layer>Duplicate Layer*) and open your first textured layer. I've used a picture of sandstone as the colour complements the autumn tones and the cracks make good texture. Click on and drag the textured image layer on to the image layer using the *Move Tool.*

2 Transform the texture Go to *Edit>Free Transform*, hold *Shift* to constrain the proportions and drag a corner widget outwards to meet the sides of your image. Press the *Tick* to commit to the adjustment. Change the texture layer's *Blend Mode* to merge it with the image layer. Here, *Overlay* was used to boost saturation.

3 Add a Layer Mask As the texture flows over the face, it can start to obscure the features. Apply a Layer Mask to the texture layer by clicking on *Create layer mask* at the bottom of the Layers palette. Select the *Brush Tool* and set a soft-edge brush with a *Opacity* set low then, using *Black* paint, brush over the face to reduce the texture.

4 Add more texture Repeat steps one to three with another texture and try out the different Blend Modes to see their effects. Here, *Multiply* was used to emphasise the lines in the tree texture. If the resulting texture is still slightly too strong, try reducing the layer's *Opacity* using the slider at the top of the Layer's palette.

5 Repeat the steps There's no rule for what textures work and how many you should use; the key is trial and error and building up the effect gradually. Here, four textures are layered, each with different Blend Modes and varying Opacity. Moving the layers in different positions within the Layers palette can also change the result.

Where can you get textures?

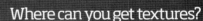

The easiest way to get texture images is to photograph them yourself: it's so easy to do and you can find them anywhere, be it a brick wall, granite table top, scrunched up paper or flaky paint on a wall. Textures are everywhere. Your other option is to download them from the internet. Sites such as deviantart.com, textureking.com and amazingtextures.com are good sources, but a quick Google search will uncover hundreds of options.

Give studio portraits a magical makeover

For a striking portrait that's a little different from the average high-key image, try this technique

Caroline Wilkinson
THIS UNCONVENTIONAL bleached-white portrait is easy to achieve and makes a great montage with various facial expressions. The technique is fairly straightforward, but its success hinges on the right preparation. The eyes, eyebrows and lips need to be striking to make the effect work, so have your model pile on the make-up and use a light-coloured powder to bleach the skin. As expected, the boys in the office were not keen on applying red lippy and eyeliner, so I used myself as the subject and set the interval timer to fire the shutter. Although your model may look like a clown, the more make-up they apply, the better the final effect.

Lighting set-up

SET-UP: Position one softbox above and in front of you, or your model, tilted down at 45°. Start by setting the light to a mid-power setting, increasing or decreasing the power to get a balance between overexposing the skin, but not the lips, eyes or eyebrows, as they will form the basis of the picture.

1 Settings If you're shooting a self-portrait, you can use a remote release or if you haven't got one, your camera's self-timer. I opted for the interval timer as it allowed me to continuously shoot a specified number of frames and it also adjusts the exposure, focus and metering before each shot. Check your DSLR's manual to find out if your camera has this facility and how to set it.

2 Be expressive Position you or your subject on a stool and set the camera up so it aligns with the face. If you're doing a self-portrait, take a few test shots and reposition yourself, and the camera, until you're framed correctly. Then pull as many faces as you can for the frames set with your interval timer. Assess the pictures, adjust the light's power, reset the interval timer and re-shoot.

3 Crop Having selected the best picture, open the image in Photoshop. As the only elements you'll need to form the picture are the facial features, select the *Crop Tool* and crop the image tightly to get rid of any distractions. Now to boost the contrast, bleaching the skin further, duplicate the layer (*Layer>Duplicate Layer*) and change the *Blend Mode* to *Overlay*.

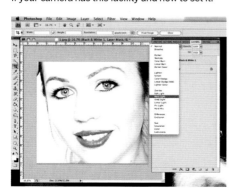

4 Add contrast Adjust Curves to bleach the face and darken the features more (*Image> Adjustments>Curves*). A clever way to boost contrast is to add a Black & White adjustment layer (*Layer>New Adjustment Layer>Black & White*), then set that adjustment layer's *Blend Mode* to *Hard Light* so that it merges with the colour image beneath.

5 Boost colours Now, to adjust the intensity of certain colours, double-click on the adjustment layer in the Layers palette and tweak the colour sliders. Try to get the skin nearly white, being careful not to turn it yellow. For this image, I've taken the Cyan and Blue to -200 to enhance the eyes, Yellow to -27 to whiten the skin and Red to -12 to boost the lips.

6 White out the face To get rid of any hair and the face's outline, go to *Layer>New>Layer* and select the *Brush Tool* and *White.* Using a large, soft brush, get rid of the remaining outlines. Now if you want to make the canvas bigger to give more space around the features, use the *Crop Tool* to select the canvas, drag the widgets to resize the canvas and then press *Enter*.

Final image

My skin's never looked so
flawless! This quirky take on
a portrait will have everyone
asking how you did it.

Give your favourite portrait a 1950's-style makeover!

Continue your creative streak after you've taken a great portrait and style yourself a piece of retro wall art using this Pop-ular Photoshop technique

Caroline Wilkinson WHEN SOMEONE SAYS Andy Warhol, probably one of the first images to pop into their head is a colourful montage of Marilyn Monroe or a Campbell's soup can. Warhol is one of the most recognised artists of the 1950's pop art movement and we're still replicating his style 60 years later, with a lot more ease since the introduction of Photoshop. When it comes to picking an image for a Photoshopped pop-art image, it's best to choose a shot with good contrast because you'll be, in effect, using the shadows as a black outline for your colours. Without good shadow detail to define the face, your subject may look like they're without a nose or mouth. If you're unsure, check the image by turning it black & white and then clicking **Image>Adjustment>Threshold** to play with the slider to see if enough detail is retained. You should also try to pick an image with a background that contrasts with the subject to make it easier to extract with the **Magic Wand Tool**. Some shots work better than others, but it's a case of trial and error. So what are you waiting for? Give your shots a new lease of life with this graphic Photoshop CS4 technique.

Be a wand wizard!
If you struggle selecting the whole background, increase or decrease the **Tolerance** level of your wand slightly and hold **Shift** while making multiple selections.

1 Create new layers Open the image and duplicate it (*Layer>Duplicate Layer*). Now go to *Layer>New Adjustment Layer> Solid Color...* and pick the colour you want your background to be. Next, click and drag this layer between the two image layers and click the top layer.

2 Colour the background Use the **Magic Wand Tool** to select the background and press the **backspace** key to reveal the coloured layer beneath. Go to **Select>Deselect,** then **Image>Adjustments> Desaturate** and then **Image>Adjustments> Threshold**, adjusting the slider to retain facial details.

3 Add blur Add a touch of blur by going to *Filter>Blur> Gaussian Blur* and setting the slider to 1px. Drag the top layer onto the **Add new layer** icon to duplicate. Select the *Paint Bucket Tool* and press the **X** key to select **White,** then click on the face. (**X** changes the foreground colour from Black to White).

4 Colour the skin Set the top layer's **Blend Mode** to **Multiply** so it interacts with the layer beneath, Click on the next layer and then add a **Solid Color...** adjustment layer, this time picking a colour for the skin. Select the **Paint Bucket Tool,** press **X**, and fill the layer with black to mask the colour.

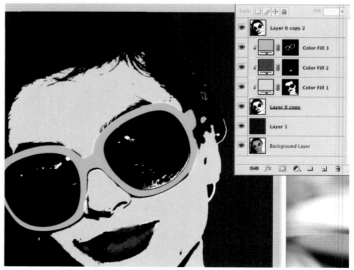

5 Link the layers Hold **Alt** and click between the second and third layer. Now select the **Brush Tool** and press **X** to choose **White** as the foreground colour and paint over the skin area. Next, using **Solid Color** adjustment layers, add as many extra colours as you need, clipping each one to the layer below it.

6 Crop the image Select the **Crop Tool** and hold down **Shift** while dragging from the top left to bottom right to create a square image. Move the square until you're happy with the crop. Double-click to complete. Select all layers except the Background layer by holding **Shift** and clicking on each layer.

Edited

7 Create the series Press *Cmd+T* to enter *Free Transform*. In the options bar at the top, change the *Width* and *Height* to 50%, and move the image to the top left of the picture. Select the *Move Tool*, hold *Alt*, drag the shot to the top right, then copy the image three times and position the boxes.

8 Change colours To change the background colours, scroll down the Layers palette to select the right layer, pick a colour and click on the selected layer with the *Paint Bucket Tool*. For other features you want to change the colour of, double click on that layer's coloured box to bring up the colour picker.

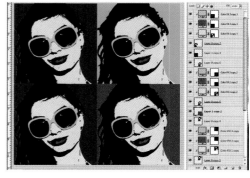

Create a rainy day portrait

Today, we forecast a heavy downpour! Give your images the illusion of rain with a few tweaks using Noise and Motion Blur…

Luke Marsh FOR MOST PHOTOGRAPHERS, shooting in the rain isn't their favourite pastime, but it can add a different dimension to your pictures. So how can you create the appearance of rain without having to actually get you or your camera gear wet? Easy, follow this technique!

Its success lies in trying to make the scene look authentic, so if your starting image is of a street scene, make sure it was taken just after it's rained, when the ground is still wet. Similarly, have your subject/s hold an umbrella to avoid the question: If it's pouring with rain, why don't they look soaking wet? An umbrella is the perfect cover-up, quite literally.

Original

ISTOCKPHOTO

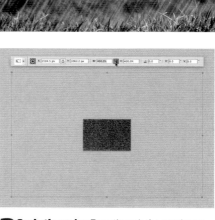

Let it snow, let it snow!

You can also adapt this rain technique to create a great snow effect! In step four, when using Motion Blur, reduce the **Distance** down to less than 10 pixels to give the appearance of drifting snow, as opposed to heavy rain. Also, having different sized flakes adds extra dimension to the scene, so go to **Layer>New>Layer via Copy** to duplicate the layer. Then **Edit>Transform>Scale** to increase the size of the new snow layer by holding **Shift** and dragging a corner widget.

1 Open your image Create a new layer above the original by going to **Layer>New Layer...** and clicking **OK** in the pop-up window. To be able to affect this layer, you need to put content into it. For this, go to **Edit>Fill...** and, under **Contents**, change **Use** to **Black** and ensure **Mode** is **Normal** and **Opacity** is 100 under the **Blending Options**.

2 Add some noise Now add noise to the new black layer by going to **Filter>Noise>Add noise...**. Select **Gaussian** under **Distribution**, and ensure that **Monochromatic** is ticked. The **Amount** of noise you need to enter will depend on the image's resolution. For large files, you will need to enter the maximum amount of 400%.

3 Scale the noise Even though the maximum amount of noise was used, the noise 'dots' need to be bigger (the higher the image resolution and size, the more this will be the case). Go to **Edit>Transform>Scale**, enter 400% in the horizontal scale field and click the link icon to scale in proportion. Double-click to apply.

Wet and wild!
Adding rain is a simple
technique, and one that
adds life and movement
to your images.

4 Create raindrops Now change the noise
layer's **Blend Mode** to **Screen**, making the
image beneath visible. The noise needs editing to
create fine raindrops, so go to **Image>
Adjustments>Levels...** and drag the black slider
all the way to the right, making the drops smaller
and allowing a better interaction with the image.

5 Blur the raindrops Use **Filter>Blur>Motion
Blur...** to add the effect of moving rain. In the
control panel, enter an **Angle** that suits your
particular image. Here, 60° was used to reflect the
position the little girl holds her umbrella. Then
enter a **Distance** that gives intermittent streaks
rather than solid lines running across the image.

6 The perfect storm The final tweaks are
done using Levels (**Image>Adjustments>
Levels...**). Move the black and white sliders to
change the rain's appearance depending on your
image. The black slider reduces the appearance of
rain from sheets to drizzle, whereas the white
slider improves the contrast of the rain.

Create 'golden hour' light

A balmy summer's evening can give a supremely flattering glow to your subject. Recreate the look using Curves and the Burn Tool…

Luke Marsh THERE'S NOTHING QUITE like a glorious summer sunset to add ambience and colour to your portrait images. However, capturing such a backlit effect can be technically challenging with tricky metering and flare posing problems, but with this simple step-by-step you can transform daytime portraits with minimal effort.

You can try this technique on any outdoor portrait, but the effect will be more dramatic the cooler the original image tones are. You rarely see clouds when there's a burning sunset so, if you can, pick an image with a generous expanse of clear blue sky in a summery location such as a flower-filled field or one with plenty of lush greenery. An image with shallow depth-of-field can also enhance the final hazy warmth of the image, though it's not essential.

Getting the Photoshop effect correct relies on you working well with Layer Masks, but the beauty of them is that they're fully editable so you can refine and re-try the technique without damaging your original image. Use black paint and a soft brush on a Layer Mask to hide effects and white paint to reveal them again, lowering the opacity for better control.

Quick find

Layer Masks
Click the *Layer Mask* icon at the bottom of the Layers palette. A thumbnail appears on the active layer in the palette.

Adjustment Layers
Click and hold on the *New Adjustment Layer* icon at the bottom of the Layers palette, scroll down the menu to find the desired adjustment.

Original

1 Create the sun First, add the sun. To do this, create a duplicate of the original image: go to *Layer>New>Layer via Copy*, then open *Filter>Render>Lens Flare...* Select *105mm Prime* from *Lens Type* and position the small cross hairs on the thumbnail preview. Finally, enter an appropriate *Brightness* amount for the image.

2 Improve the face The flare strength means the subject's face appears very burnt out. To solve this, add a Layer Mask by clicking the icon in the Layers palette. Select a soft-edged brush, set to *Black*, with an *Opacity* of around 20%, and paint over the subject to reduce the effects of the flare, without removing it completely.

3 Sunset gradient In the toolbar, make sure the background colour is *White*, then click on the foreground colour icon. In the Color Picker, change to a sunset colour. Now click on the *Add new adjustment layer* icon in the Layers palette and select *Gradient*... Set *Style* to *Linear* and tick *Reverse*, so the gradient runs from top to bottom.

Hello sunshine!
Give your images the Midas touch by adding a gorgeous sunset to your shots.

4 Tweak the gradient Change the *Blend Mode* to *Color*. To reduce the colour tint on the subject, use a Layer Mask, as in step 2. A gradient adjustment layer has a Layer Mask by default, so click on it in the Layers palette, select a medium soft-edged brush, set to *Black*, with *Opacity* at 20%, and begin work on the subject.

5 Use Curves Click the *Add new adjustment layer* icon and choose *Curves*... Now you can create an 'S' curve or choose *Strong Contrast* from the *Preset* menu and click *OK*. The effect can be harsh on the subject's face, so create a Layer Mask and reduce the effects by using the *Brush Tool* set to *Black*, as in the previous step.

6 Burn the foreground To finish, click on the duplicate image layer that holds the flare, ensuring the image thumbnail is active and not the Layer Mask. Select the *Burn Tool* and, using a large soft-edged brush with *Opacity* set to about 20%, begin to work around the foreground of the image to darken it off, adding depth to the image.

Black & white portraits

When shooting portraits to convert to monochrome, there are a few factors that you need to consider...

THE STRENGTH OF a monochromatic picture is determined by its raw components: form, composition and tonal range all have to be at their strongest. As well as geometry, there has to be a good balance of tones throughout the picture so that the eye is not forced to linger on areas that are too black or white heavy and encourage it to move around the whole image. It's amazing how many brilliant colour images fail when they are turned into monochrome and how many images that don't work in colour can come to life as a black & white conversion!

In order to ensure that you take a picture with the potential for black & white, you have to visualise the scene in mono – and this isn't an easy thing to do. For example, if you have a subject wearing a blue coat and they stand against green foliage, the tones will be very similar in black & white due to the limited tonal separation, thus losing the depth between foreground and background. In a colour image, you can see the depth because of the disparity between the green and blue, but in mono that same image will look flat. The distinction between relative lightness and darkness is important – you have to think about tonality that much more. There is a monochromatic filter on the market that can help. You put it to your eye and, while it doesn't remove colour entirely, it does reduce it so that you can evaluate the scene's potential based on its geometry and tonality.

To capture your best black & white pictures, you need to get used to 'seeing' in a colourless world and pick your model and background appropriately. For example, if your location has green foliage you should choose a model with blonde rather than brown hair. Blonde hair will look that much lighter in monochrome and provide better separation from this sort of background. If you have to work with a specific model, you might think about moving them across to a different background if things don't look tonally distinct, or perhaps change their clothes if background choice is limited.

Mono magic
While this colour image is striking, as a black & white, its composition and tonal range has made it even more dynamic and visually pleasing.

Black & white plug-ins

Silver Efex Pro 2 €199.95 (around £175)
Nik Software / www.niksoftware.com
A fully-featured plug-in for Photoshop, Elements, Lightroom and Aperture that delivers top-quality conversions. The interface borrows much from the traditional darkroom, including the ability to simulate black & white films and manipulate parts of the picture selectively with Control Points. Expensive but very powerful.

Black & White Studio €30 (around £26)
Power Retouche / www.powerretouche.com
Affordable and full of features, Black & White Studio offers a large number of adjustable parameters, including colour sensitivity. Exposure as well as highlight and shadow detail can be controlled individually, and 'print quality' can be adjusted to emulate different contrast grades of photographic paper.

BW Workflow Pro $19.90 (around £12)
Fred Miranda / www.fredmiranda.com
The principal behind this plug-in is control – and lots of it. You can take charge over literally every aspect of your mono conversion with BW Workflow Pro, from coloured filters to duotone and tritone presets. Even dynamic range is handled with ease, and the plug-in can simulate black & white infrared photography too.

BJORN THOMASSEN

The top ten ways of converting colour to monochrome

There is more than one way to convert a photograph to black & white. Some are easy, others more involved. Some allow no control at all, others give more than you could ever want. Here are ten Photoshop techniques to get you started – if you know of any more, please do let us know!

1) Grayscale mode Switching from RGB to Grayscale mode (*Image>Mode>Grayscale*) dumps all colour information. For this very reason, we wouldn't recommend this method as it restricts your scope for editing.

2) Desaturate In the *Image> Adjustments* menu, select *Desaturate* to drain the colour from your image in one click.

3) Convert to B&W A Black & White command, found in the *Image>Adjustments* menu is a more controllable way to turn to mono. You can add it as an Adjustment Layer too.

4) Channel Mixer Choose *Image>Adjustments>Channel Mixer*. Tick the *Monochrome* box and now you can play with colour sensitivities with the Red, Green and Blue sliders.

5) Just one channel Looking at just one channel will give you a black & white view. Choose the one that gives the best result from the Channels palette (*Windows>Channels*).

6) Gradient Map Often discovered by mistake as it's the next command down from Channel Mixer in the *Image> Adjustments* menu, the Gradient Map can be used to change an image to pure black & white.

7) Hue/Saturation A Hue/ Saturation adjustment layer (*Layer>New Adjustment Layer >Hue/Saturation*) with the saturation slider moved to the left removes colour from your image. And it's non-destructive too.

8) LAB Colour In LAB colour mode (*Image>Mode>LAB*) choose either A or B from the *Channels* palette. Both will give you a mono result.

9) Raw files In Adobe Camera Raw, click the *HSL* tab and you'll be presented with colour sensitivity sliders so that you can mimic the effect of using coloured optical filters.

10) Duotone Not strictly mono, but we wanted to include it here anyway. Duotone images use black, white and an extra colour for a subtle tint. With a Grayscale image choose *Image>Mode> Duotone* and experiment or try one of the built-in presets.

Create a film noir portrait

Adding grain to a black & white portrait can provide a timeless film feel. Find out how to shoot a gritty and nostalgic low-key portrait

Caroline Wilkinson THERE ARE FEW instances when we'd ask you to try and light a portrait for deep shadows and high contrast, but it seems to suit low-key monochrome, adding drama and mystery. We'd also normally advise you to steer clear of digital noise because its grain can ruin a shot, but when trying to simulate an old black & white film image, there's nothing quite like grain to add authenticity.

As opposed to a high-key portrait that's very clean and bright with light tones, a low-key portrait is gritty and moody with predominantly dark tones. It's actually quite easy to accomplish, as you only need one light and don't have to be overly concerned with unflattering shadows. You don't need studioflash either, you can use window light instead, but for the best results use a black or dark backdrop so that there's minimal highlights in the image. If you position your subject next to a window, use a net curtain to soften the light so it's more flattering.

If working with natural light, you'll probably use aperture-priority, so it's a good idea to bracket the exposures or add a couple of stops of negative exposure compensation override the metering system, which will render the predominantly dark scene as a mid-tone. You want a shot that has lit elements exposed while the rest of the image is in the dark.

For this step-by-step, I've used a single Elinchrom D-Lite 4IT head with a softbox. While you could set your camera to a high ISO to increase digital noise, you'll be better to apply grain using Photoshop to record a sharper result. To add to the 1920's film effect, I asked my model to wear a hat for added texture and interest and to wear dark clothes so that the attention is drawn to her face and the lighting sharply falls off into blackness.

As well as adding noise in Photoshop, there are also a lot of plug-in filters available, including the brilliant Silver Efex Pro package by Nik Software that offer you a greater level of control and creativity over your film noir image.

Third-party plug-in filters

Nik Color Efex Pro 3.0 Complete enables you to apply a Film Effect and Film Grain to your pictures with one or two clicks. With this software, simply open the image in Photoshop and scroll down the *Filters* menu to Nik Software to access a huge selection of filter options. You can then select *Film Grain* and be more specific about the size and saturation of grain you introduce to the highlights, shadows and mid-tones. And in Nik Silver Efex Pro 2, under *Film Effects*, you can pick from a list of different film types at various ISOs or control the level of grain manually.
www.niksoftware.com

Before | After

1 Set up Position the subject a few metres from the backdrop so that none of the light from the softbox falls on it, turning it grey or highlighting wrinkles and creases. Switch your camera to manual mode and set the shutter speed to 1/250sec (or whatever your camera's flash sync speed is) and the ISO to its lowest rating. You'll need to adjust the aperture to control how the subject is exposed.

2 Take a test shot Position the studioflash 45° to the side and pointing down on the subject. Start with it about a metre away, set to its lowest power. Take a meter reading from the face (I got f/5.6) and a test shot, making sure you're happy with how the shadows fall on the face. At this point the shadows won't be strong enough, but you have your starting point. Now stop the aperture down.

Wrong | Right

3 Experiment Varying the light's distance from the subject as well as the aperture will limit the light that reaches the face and can help achieve a better effect. Be watchful of where the light falls on the subject though – the eyes are important in a portrait, so make sure these are well exposed. I found between f/10 and f/13 worked well.

4 Open in ACR Open your favourite image in Adobe Camera Raw and make the adjustments you feel you need to under the *Basic* tab, then switch to the *HSL/Grayscale* tab and click on *Convert to Grayscale*. You can then adjust the colour sliders to tweak the tones. In this case the *Orange* slider improved the skin tone.

5 Clean up the image Once you're happy with your picture, click *OK* to open it in Photoshop. Apply any cropping that you require and then duplicate the layer (*Layer> Duplicate Layer*) and work on it using the *Healing Brush* and *Clone Stamp Tool* to get rid of any blemishes. You're now ready to add the grain.

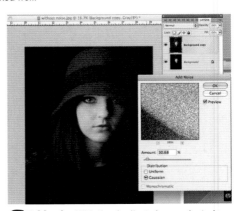

6 Add noise With the duplicate layer selected, go to *Filter>Noise>Add Noise* to open the *Add Noise* dialogue box. The Gaussian distribution will have a much stronger effect than Uniform and places random noise across the image, which is closer to what film does. Adjust the *Amount* slider until you're happy with the level of noise.

Final image
As the noise will be added to the shadows, you'll probably find that the blacks turn slightly grey. To correct this, go to *Layer>New Adjustment Layer>Brightness/ Contrast* and then adjust the *Contrast* slider slightly.

Learn how to retouch your portraits like a pro

Always wanted to create polished portraits like the professionals? Well now's your chance. The best-kept secrets of retouching are disclosed in this guide from some of the world's leading retouchers – read on to find out how to enhance the natural beauty of your subjects with expert tutorials and advice

OFTEN THE DIFFERENCE between average portraits and the polished images that you see by high-end pros or in glossy magazines is not only photographic prowess, but the skill of the retoucher, or lack thereof. In many respects, the taking of a portrait is just one step towards a finished picture, but great lighting and photography are fundamental as Photoshop is not a miracle worker: it's an enhancement tool – and a powerful one at that. It can transform good photos to great, images with impact, but you need a quality picture to begin with to get the most from post-production. While how you originally light the subject doesn't affect retouching, the lighting should be as close as you can get it to the finished look and your exposure needs to be spot-on: if you can get the skin looking light and bright, rather than a muddy tone, retouching is going to be a lot easier. If you have to lighten up pixels, you'll have noise issues, the colour won't be as good and it'll take a lot longer to get a half-decent result. Some photographers mistakenly start with a bad image, thinking they can transform it in Photoshop, but apply so much manipulation that the picture loses any sense of realism.

There are some other things you can do to make retouching easier. Make sure you shoot in Raw rather than JPEG. Make-up is helpful, too: apply foundation that's the right tone for the skin to avoid any lines between the face and neck, as well as a light dusting of powder to get rid of shine caused by the heat of the studio lights. Lipstick should be applied perfectly: make sure the lips are sculpted properly and there's no bleeding over the edges of the mouth and the eye make-up shapes the eyes. Lighting and smoothing are essential for beautiful hair. Split ends are a nightmare to retouch, so try to make sure the hair is in good condition before you start and preferably lit well to create highlights. The more highlights there are to begin with, the easier they will be to draw out during editing.

Before you start retouching, you need to calibrate your monitor (we'd recommend X-Rite's i1Match, Datacolor's Spyder3 Elite or Pantone hueyPRO for easy-to-use calibration devices). Skipping this step could mean your printed image looks nothing like it did on screen and those hours of colour refinement and tonal tweaks were wasted. Then plan what you want to do to the image – it should stop you from over or under-processing areas – make yourself a coffee and be prepared for a long time in front of your monitor. The most polished and subtle retouching takes an abundance of time, an eye for detail and plenty of patience to ensure natural-looking results. Retouching is not about changing a model beyond recognition or transforming them into a Barbie doll; you should be trying to enhance features and work with the person's natural beauty so the portrait presents the very best version of them and improves the overall image impact.

Start by assessing the overall quality of the skin: blemishes, under-eye 'bags', how even the colour is, the cleanliness of the make-up,

Original

deep-set wrinkles, crow's feet and unwanted highlights created by shiny skin. Next, address the features: do the eyebrows need to be neatened? Can the shape be improved or stray hairs eliminated? Could the eyes be brightened and the colour intensified? Is the nose a too wide or the teeth a little stained? There is so much that can be refined that even small tweaks make a huge improvement.

For the final image to look great, you need to work on the details, and that means zooming in and working on areas of pixels close up. Use lots of layers, but keep them organised and remember to save, save, save: it's easy to get engrossed and forget. Once you're finished, save the layered image as a .PSD file in case you want to come back to it, but also flatten the layers (**Image>Flatten Image**) and save the image as a TIFF to compress the enormous file size for print. This article was produced with the advice and insight of professional retouchers Fay Bacon, Amy Dresser and Chanelle Segerius-Bruce.

Retouching software

While manually retouching portraits offers unlimited control, there are a few automated software packages and plug-ins for Adobe products dedicated to retouching. If you're wanting one-click wonders with automated results, then check out these three: they're not cheap additions to your arsenal, so we'd advise giving each of them a trial run first in combination with these Photoshop techniques to see which ones you prefer.

● **Portrait Professional 10**
Free trial / starting from £64.95
www.portraitprofessional.com

● **Portraiture 2**
Free 15-day trial / $199.95
www.imagenomic.com

● **Perfect Portrait 1**
Free 30-day trial / $99.95
www.ononesoftware.com

Edited

Real beauty

Notice how the skin looks flawless, but you can still see the natural texture, pores and lines in the skin. To see how this is done, turn to page 123.

Photoshop fundamentals

This entire guide is based on techniques that you can do in Photoshop CS3, 4, 5 and, in some cases, Elements 10, but it's also been written for Macintosh users, so a few of the shortcuts might be different for PC users. As some of the tutorials are already quite detailed, we've kept them as concise as possible by avoiding explanations of the tools and features. If you're unsure of how to access or use a feature, refer back to this list.

● **Organisation:** You may notice in the final tutorial (page 119) that Amy Dresser groups her layers into folders; she does this to aid organisation. If you want to do the same thing, click on the **Create New Group** icon at the bottom of the Layers palette (looks like a folder), give the folder a name and then click and drag the appropriate layers into the folder. You can hide the layers in the folder by clicking on the arrow next to the group layer. Re. Mac v PC: Substitute **Cmd** (Mac) for **Ctrl** (PC) and **Option** (Mac) for **Alt** (PC).

● **Layers:** Layers are at the heart of successful retouching as they allow you to apply edits to separate layers so that you can return and edit them at any stage. There are three types of layers: a new layer (**Layer>New**), which is empty; an Adjustment Layer (see below) that enables you to apply non-destructive edits to your image, like contrast and colour adjustments; and duplicate layers (**Layer>Duplicate**), which allow you to create an identical copy of a layer and its contents.

● **Layer Mask:** Use this to edit adjustments on a layer. Use the **Brush Tool** with **Black** paint to brush over areas to hide or minimise the adjustment and White paint to reveal it again. Vary the opacity of the brush to adjust the strength of the edit. You can add a Layer Mask to a layer by clicking on the **Add New Layer Mask** icon at the bottom of the Layers palette or going to (**Layer>Layer Mask> Reveal all/Hide all**). By default, the Layer Mask should be white, so you should use **Black** paint to hide the adjustment on areas of the image. You can also invert the Layer Mask (**Command & I**) to fill it with Black to hide the entire adjustment and then use **White** paint to selectively reveal adjusted areas in the image you want to show. To delete a Layer Mask, click on the link symbol to disconnect it from the layer and drag to the trash.

● **New Adjustment Layer:** As your image editing should be carried out in stages and be non-destructive (never irrevocably affecting the original image in case you need to use it again), Adjustment Layers are fundamental to your workflow. You can access them either via **Layer>New Adjustment Layer** or by clicking on the **Add New Adjustment Layer** icon at the bottom of the Layers palette. Each Adjustment Layer has a Layer Mask attached, allowing you to use the **Brush Tool** to edit the adjustment on areas of the image.

● **Blend modes:** Accessible via the **Blend Mode** menu at the top of the Layers palette, these modes dictate how the layer its applied to 'blends' with the layer below it.

● **Clone Stamp Tool:** One of the most used tools in Photoshop when it comes to retouching, the Clone Stamp copies pixels from one area of an image and replaces them in another. It works by pressing Alt on the area you want to copy from and then clicking on the area you want to replace, like a spot or blemish. We'd advise picking a 'source' area close to the area you want to replace for similar skin tones. Once you've selected this tool from the toolbar, you can adjust the size of the Clone Stamp and its opacity from the Options bar. We suggest, unless you're working on hairs where 100% opacity and a hard edge is necessary, set the **Opacity** slider to around 20% with 0% **Hardness** and gradually build up the effect for smoother and more forgiving results.

● **Liquify:** Useful for sculpting the face, body and hair, Liquify can be a tricky tool to control, so use it carefully and as described in this guide, or see the *Photoshop for Photographers* 3rd Edition MagBook (www.magbooks.com) for an in-depth look at how to use it. To use it, go to **Filter>Liquify**.

● **Smart Object:** If you're opening a file you've edited in Adobe Camera Raw (ACR), we'd suggest opening it as a Smart Object by holding down **Shift** to change the **Open** button to **Open Object**. At any point now, you can re-edit the Raw file by double-clicking on the image layer in Photoshop.

Using a graphics tablet & stylus

Making selections can be made much easier with a pressure-sensitive graphics tablet such as Wacom's Bamboo or Intuos4 (the latter is for the advanced users in need of more control over their editing). With practice, they're easier and more versatile than a mouse as they're ergonomically better for drawing. You can also assign shortcuts to different pressure points on the pen, such as brush size and feather. For details, visit: www.wacom.com

Skin

Learn the techniques that help
the professionals to get portraits
with picture-perfect skin

THE CLASSIC MISTAKE when retouching is to
over-process the skin, hiding the natural
pores, hair and texture. Applying Gaussian
blur to soften the skin is a popular technique
with amateur photographers as it's quick and
easy to do, but it's also easy to 'overdo',
causing you to lose the sculpting and fine
details on the face that make it look natural.

We'd advise spending as much time as
possible retouching the skin for the best
results and there are several techniques to try,
depending on how much time you've got and
how dramatic you want the finish to be. In this
section, we've delved straight in to Photoshop,
but if you flick over a few pages to our
complete workflow tutorial by Annie
Leibovitz's retoucher, Amy Dresser, you can
see how to start retouching images from Raw
in Adobe Camera Raw (ACR). Amy
concentrates on small, selective tonal and
colour adjustments that even out the skin tone
for flawless results. It's an advanced technique
that takes practice to perfect and experience
in Photoshop, but here are a few simpler steps
to get you started and alone can dramatically
improve your portraits.

Pro tip: Fay Bacon

■ **Patch Tool and Clone Stamp Tool**
Firstly, I use the *Patch Tool* to remove
large blemishes and lines. Duplicate
the image layer and then 'patch' away
any lines. Add a Layer Mask and 'paint'
over the areas you've 'patched' with a
low opacity brush to bring back some
of the texture, lines and wrinkles to a
level that you want them visible. When
it comes to reducing dark under-eye circles,
I use the *Clone Stamp Tool* with the *Opacity* set
to around 20% and lightly blend in the new skin.
You can go over it more until you get your desired
coverage and use a Layer Mask to reveal details
if you overdo it. To apply the skin to an empty
layer from the image layer, make sure *Sample* is
set to *All Layers*.

Rapid retouching

1) Blemishes and wrinkles: Use the *Healing
Brush* and *Clone Stamp Tool* (set to a large,
soft brush with low opacity) to reduce the
appearance of wrinkles and blemishes. Click
the *Fade* command (*Edit>Fade*) after each
adjustment to bring texture back, gradually
building up coverage. The *Healing Brush Tool*
is very good at covering wrinkles and if you set
the Clone Stamp Tool's *Blend Mode* to *Lighten*,
it works well to brighten as well as soften the
skin. Make sure you work on a new layer for each
major adjustment, so you can adjust or delete
stages with ease.

2) Dark under-eye circles: Apply a *Curves*
or *Levels* adjustment layer and brighten the
image, focusing on the under-eye area. Invert
the attached Layer Mask to hide the adjustment
and use the *Brush Tool* with *White* paint to reveal
the under-eye areas. You can then reduce the
Opacity of that layer if the under-eyes look too
bright compared to the rest of the face.

Airbrush with Gaussian blur

1) Remove blemishes
Here we've used the *Patch
Tool* on a duplicate layer
and then the *Clone Stamp
Tool* with a new layer to
remove obvious marks,
reduce the wrinkles and
smooth out the skin.

1) Adjust colour
Use the *Lasso Tool* with
a generous feather to
select sections of the skin
where the colour needs
to be adjusted using the
Channels in a *Curves*
adjustment layer.

1) Apply blur
Select all your layers and
click *Command+Alt+Shift
+E* to create a combined
copy of all the layers. Go
to *Filter>Blur> Gaussian
Blur* and set a blur of
between 20 and 30.

1) Reveal details
Add a Layer Mask and
invert it, then use the
Brush Tool with an
Opacity of 20% to brush
over the skin to smooth it.
Avoid areas like the eyes,
mouth and nostrils.

**Top Tip: Enhance the
highlights to add sheen**
Create a duplicate layer
and use the *Dodge Tool*, set
to a low *Exposure* (2-3%)
and a soft, medium-sized
brush to enhance what
natural highlights there
are. Gradually build up the
effect, varying the *Range*
between *Highlights* and
Midtones to brighten areas
of the face and to create
highlights where there
might not be any to sculpt
the face. Remember to
work on a duplicate layer,
in case you need to revert
back to the original image
or reduce the opacity of the
layer to control the effect.

Features

Enhance your subject's facial features with these simple, yet very effective, steps

THE EYES, TEETH, LIPS AND NOSE all require similar amounts of attention, and are just as important as the skin when it comes to trying to make a portrait more beautiful. Here are a few pro techniques to try:

Eyes & teeth

1) Use the Dodge Tool: Duplicate the image layer so you're not working on the original image's pixels. Select a brush *Size* a little smaller than the whites of the eyes, set the *Range* to *Midtone* and the *Exposure* to around 2-3%, then 'brush' over the whites of the eyes and teeth. You only want to go a couple of shades brighter, so be careful as they can quickly look unnatural.

2) Use Hue/Saturation: Apply a *Hue/Saturation* adjustment layer and reduce the *Reds* and *Yellows*, then use the Layer Mask to hide the adjustment, just revealing the eyes and teeth. Next, select the eyes with the *Lasso Tool* and a *Feather* of 3px or 4px. Then apply a *Curves* adjustment layer and create an 'S' curve to boost the contrast in the eye.

3) Use Selective Color: Select the eye or the teeth with the *Lasso Tool* and apply a small *Feather* of 10px to soften the edges. Then add a *Selective Color* adjustment layer and click on the drop-down menu at the top of the dialogue box, select *Neutral* and adjust the sliders until you see the area/s selected gradually whiten. Do the same with *Whites*.

IMAGES ISTOCK PHOTO

Pro tip: Chanelle Segerius-Bruce

■ Add a soft catchlight
As some eyes are quite deep-set, they often need a bit of brightening and life added. One way is to use a *Curves* adjustment layer to lighten the eye, then invert the Layer Mask and use the *Brush Tool* to paint in a half-moon shape, using *White* paint underneath the pupil to create a highlight similar to what you'd get if you'd used a reflector.

Change eye colour

Use the *Lasso Tool* to draw around the iris and set a small feather to soften the edges. Add a *Selective Color* adjustment layer and then adjust the sliders via the colours/tones offered in the drop-down menu to alter the colour of the eye to suit your subject or image. Select the eye again in the same way, but this time apply a *Hue/Saturation* adjustment layer and make small tweaks to the intensity of the colour. Finally, add a *Curves* adjustment layer, if necessary, to boost contrast and enhance that twinkle!

Reshape the nose

1) Slimming a nose: The nose can be a very prominent feature and while we don't suggest you completely reconstruct someone's nose, as it's a key feature of their face, you can minimise its distraction from the eyes with a few simple tricks. Access Liquify (*Filter>Liquify*) and select the *Forward Warp Tool*, set a low *Density* and *Pressure* and a brush *Size* appropriate for the size of the nose, and carefully push in the side of the nose and nostrils.

Editing lips

2) Make fuller lips: Once again access *Liquify*, but this time select the *Bloat Tool* with a low *Rate* and *Pressure*, then make small clicks along the inside of the lips to make them 'bloat'. Remember: less is more, so don't attempt to make it look like bad collagen injections – it won't flatter any subject!

3) Enrich the natural colour: Create a new layer and paint *Black* on top of your model's lips using the *Brush Tool* (you can use any colour here, but Black is good for enriching the natural lip colour of your model). Next, click *Filter>Blur>Gaussian Blur* and set it to 4px to smooth the edges. Change the layer's *Blend Mode* to *Soft Light* and reduce the *Opacity*, if necessary. Now use the *Dodge Tool* on the image layer, with its *Range* set to *Highlights*, and brush over the top of the lips to improve the highlights and give them a glossy appearance.

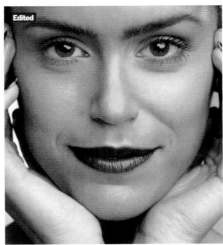

How to apply make-up

Ideally, make-up should be applied correctly before taking a picture. If not, a digital makeover can enhance features.

1) Create the base Do what skin retouching you need to. Here, the model's lips are quite chapped, so we've zoomed in close and used the *Clone Stamp Tool* to smooth out the area, and then enhanced the colour. We used a different image layer for every adjustment in case we needed to go back to edit later.

2) Eyeliner Create a new layer and zoom into the first eye so it fills the screen, select a small brush with *Black* paint and draw around the edge of the eye to add definition. Change the layer's *Blend Mode* to *Soft Light* and reduce its *Opacity*, if necessary. You can use the same technique to draw in eyelashes, too.

3) Eyeshadow Create another new layer and, using a larger, soft brush, 'paint' over the eyelid and slightly under the eye with your chosen *Foreground Color*. Then change the *Blend Mode* to *Soft Light* or *Color Burn*, reducing the *Opacity* of the layer to suit. Use *Hue/Saturation* to adjust colour.

4) Enhance the eyes Give the eye more impact by selecting the iris with the *Lasso Tool* and then add a *Selective Color adjustment layer* and adjust the sliders to suit the subject. Brighten the whites using the *Dodge Tool* as previously explained or by using a *Curves* adjustment layer.

5) Blush Pick your colour for the cheeks and, using a soft, large brush, 'paint' over the cheekbone area onto a new layer. Next, go to *Filter>Blur>Gaussian Blur* and set a *Radius* of 40 pixels to drastically soften the edges. Click *OK*. Change the layer's *Blend Mode* to *Color Burn* or *Linear Burn*.

6) Skin tone To warm up a cool skin tone, apply a *Photo Filter adjustment layer* and set *Warming Filter*, adjusting the *Density* slider to control intensity. Invert the *Layer Mask* and reveal the areas of skin you want affected by the adjustment, reducing the layer's *Opacity*.

Hair

Get glossy, healthy hair with this tutorial

YOU'D BE AMAZED at the time it takes to retouch hair at a professional standard; we're talking days or weeks for those retouchers preparing a picture for a shampoo commercial or competition. For straight hair, they would literally have to clone each stray hair so it was straight using a very hard 2px brush set to 100% opacity. You also have to reduce the amount of flyaway hairs to smooth out the surface, but if you eliminate too many, the hair can end up looking like a helmet.

To make the hair look fuller and thicker, some retouchers may even composite hair from various different shots into the picture and morph them together using layers and Layer Masks. It can be a huge amount of work, which is why we've picked up a few tips from our professional contributors, including retoucher Chanelle Segerius-Bruce (www.retouchme.co.uk), who has retouched images for Pantene campaigns and The Body Shop.

Neatening up hair

To reduce those niggly little flyaway strands and smooth out the surface of the hair, start by adding an empty new layer and set the layer's *Blend Mode* to *Darken*. Now select the *Clone Stamp Tool*, set the *Hardness* to *100%*, *Opacity* to *100%* and the *Blend Mode* to *Darken*, too. Use a small brush, big enough to cover the strand of hair, and take a sample from the area just next to it and clone over the strand. While the Darken blend mode works on light flyaway hairs, if the strands are dark, set the *Blend Mode* for the layer and brush to *Lighten* instead. To get rid of hairs entirely, use the same technique by setting the *Blend Mode* to *Normal*.

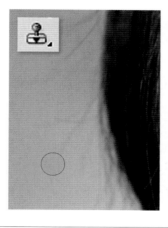

Change hair colour

Only alter colour a few shades from the original: dramatic changes make it difficult to target flyaway hair

1) The easiest way to select the hair is to use *Quick Mask Mode* (*Select>Edit* in Quick Mask Mode) and 'paint' over the hair area. When you're done, click *Select>Edit* in Quick Mask Mode again to remove the red mask and reveal the selection.

2) Create a new layer and use the *Brush Tool* loaded with your choice of colour. 'Paint' over the selection onto the empty new layer and change the *Blend Mode* to *Soft Light* to merge the colour with the texture and natural colour of the hair.

3) The tricky part is when it comes to targeting missed stray hairs of the original colour. Zoom in close and use a small brush to edit the obvious hairs and then use a *Layer Mask* to remove colour where needed.

Want shampoo commercial-worthy hair? Then follow these few easy steps...

1) Boost contrast Add a *Curves adjustment layer* and boost the *contrast* (concentrating on bringing out the natural highlights in the hair), click *OK*. Now invert the attached *Layer Mask* (*command & I*) to fill it with *black*, hiding the adjustment.

2) Refine Using the *Brush Tool* on the Layer Mask, 'paint' over the natural highlights to strengthen them. Reduce the *Opacity* of the adjustment layer if needed and switch the layer's visibility on and off to see the effects and to help judge where the highlights are.

3) Dodge Next, duplicate the image layer and select the *Dodge Tool*. With a large brush, target the highlights with an *Exposure* of *10-15%*, varying the *Range* between *Midtones* and *Highlights*. Reduce the layer's *Opacity* if you overdo it slightly.

4) Sharpen Duplicate the layer again and apply a *High Pass filter* (*Filter>High Pass*) set to *5px* and change the layer's *Blend Mode* to *Soft Light*. As High Pass can be a little harsh on skin, add a *Layer Mask* and hide the skin, leaving only the hair looking crisper.

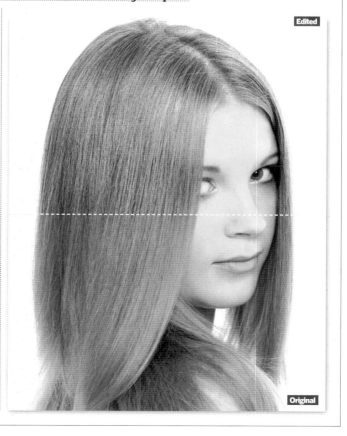

Body shape

Learn the trade tricks for sculpting a body with Liquify

LIQUIFY IS USUALLY the first tool to hand for retouchers wanting to edit a person's body, whether it be shrinking or elongating a waist, increasing breast or bicep size, slimming legs or lumps and bumps. High-end retoucher Fay Bacon (www.celebritypublicity.co.uk / www.ukmodelfolios.co.uk), who has worked on images of models for many high-profile photographers, explains how she performs subtle body sculpting.

Elongate legs

1) Lengthen legs: To elongate the legs, I select the bottom half of the image beneath the knees using the *Rectangular Marquee Tool* and then go to *Edit>Transform* and pull the whole image down to extend it while keeping the natural proportions. In this image, there wasn't enough space between the feet and the bottom part of the picture, so I increased the height of the canvas (*Image>Canvas Size*) by 4cm, then lengthened the legs. You also need to be careful not to distort the background if it's busy, as you may be forced to rebuild it using the *Clone Stamp Tool* if it stretches too much.

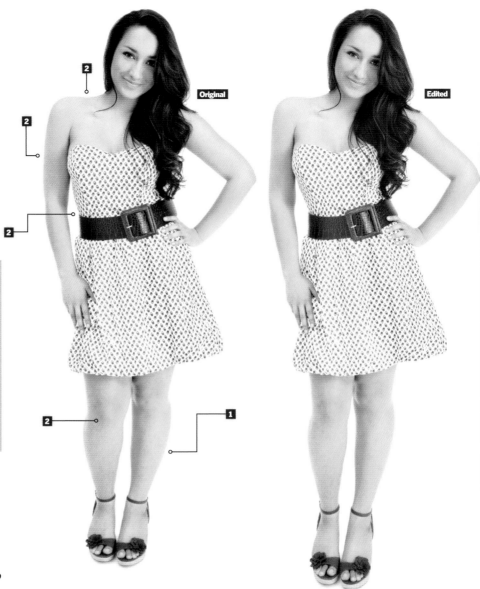

Original

Edited

2) A nip and tuck: I open the image in Liquify, set the *Brush Size* to around 300, *Density* to 12 and *Pressure* to 54, then using the *Forward Warp Tool*, push the lines of the legs and thighs in to slim them a little. I then push in the waist on either side and push down the area between the neck and shoulder (the slimmer you are, the more this area naturally curves). I then shrink the *Brush Size* and concentrate around the tops of the arms and elbow to make them appear slightly more toned. To correct any mistakes, use the *Reconstruct Tool* to brush over edited areas to revert them back to their original state.

Breasts & muscles

Select the area you want to adjust with the *Lasso Tool* and set a *Feather* of around 20px to soften the edges of the adjustment. Then go to *Filter> Distort>Spherize* and move the slider to around 50% to enlarge and lift the selection out of the image for more dimensionality.

Pro tip: Fay Bacon

■ **Clone Stamp Tool**
If there are body parts you want to adjust that are quite close together (like the arm and the waist) use the *Clone Stamp Tool* to sculpt the area by sampling the background, instead of Liquify, as this can distort the picture. You may need to adjust or add the shadows in the area you've sculpted for it to look natural.

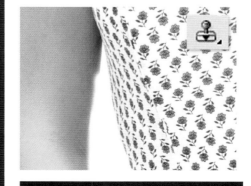

The professional solution

LA-based retoucher Amy Dresser is highly regarded in the industry for her signature style. Here, she reveals her workflow and trade secrets

Original

AMY DRESSER IS A FREELANCE RETOUCHER for numerous professional photographers and, perhaps most notably, was Jill Greenberg's full-time retoucher. Photographers come to her specifically for her signature technique, which she describes as "straddling perfection and realism". While she concentrates on achieving clean skin, she's very careful to retain the reality of the person by using tiny polishing adjustments rather than the grand skin bleaching used by many retouchers.

A lot of her work is based on refining skin colour by making small selections and adjustments using the Red, Green and Blue Channels in a Curves adjustment layer, with the aim to make the skin the same overall tone and saturation for a flawless, even finish.

Amy starts by selecting a 'hero' area on the face – an area she wants to make everything else match – and then uses her fine-tuned eye to target small areas that need to be adjusted, like the pinks of the cheeks or lightness on the forehead. It's this process that sets her apart from many other professional retouchers, as it demands several hours of careful work.

Shooting and processing Raw files gives you a lot more flexibility when it comes to preparing an image for retouching, but for the best results, use Adobe Camera Raw (ACR) to create a solid base, then take it into Photoshop where you can control small sections and add her sought-after professional sheen that makes the face more three-dimensional. To see more of Amy's astonishing work, visit: www.amydresser.com

1 Edit in Raw Start with the *Exposure* slider and work down: *Exposure* and *Fill Light* are the most important to me. There's not a correct adjustment: go with what looks right and gives you a solid start. Adjust the *Temperature* and *Tint* sliders last, as these tend to influence the mood of the image and are more negotiable. If the skin and hair look best at different settings, consider processing two versions and composite the files.

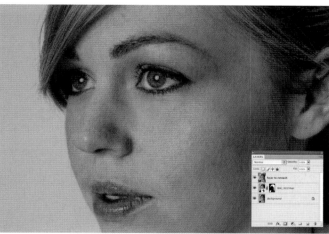

2 Composite with smart objects If the image was processed more than once, you need to combine these separate images into one. To do this, open each file as Smart Objects and drag each exposure on top of the base exposure. Then use a Layer Mask to hide parts of the images you don't want to show. Once finished, press *shift+option+command+E* to combine the files into a new base layer, which you'll use for retouching.

3 Adjust global colour Start with a few global colour adjustments to bring out or minimise details in the skin – both desirable and undesirable. Use what Adjustment Layer you're comfortable with: I prefer Curves and slightly adjust the RGB and the individual Channels, accessible via the drop-down menu. There's no right or wrong: it's a matter of personal taste. I also slightly desaturate the image using a *Hue/Saturation* adjustment layer.

Before

After

4 Clone Remove any large distractions, like stray hairs, specks, lint or acne, using the *Clone Tool* with its *Opacity* set to 100% on your 'layer to retouch'. Zoom in closer to the image to make precise adjustments easier. Resist the urge to eliminate everything you see, just things that might jump to your attention if you squint or blur your vision. See if you can limit yourself to just five minutes on this step.

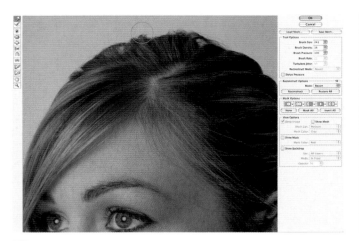

5 Use Liquify Tame any bumps in the hair using Liquify's *Forward Warp Tool* (you can also use this on bulges in clothing, too, but avoid using it on people). Use a combination of a big brush with one or two pushes, and smaller brushes with several smaller pushes. It's a very slippery tool, so don't be ashamed to undo (*command+Z*) as often as needed. This step is not always necessary and one I sometimes skip.

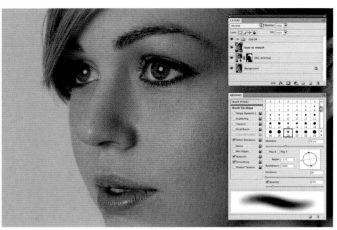

6 Dodge and burn Refine skin tone and texture using the Dodge and Burn Tools. Use an ultra-soft brush set to 3% *Exposure*, *Range*: Midtones with *Protect Tones* unticked (CS5 only). 'Dodge' spots and small areas that stand out as being too dark, and 'burn' spots and small areas that stand out as being too light with a brush about the size of the spot. With much larger brushes, use these tools to refine the contours of the face as well.

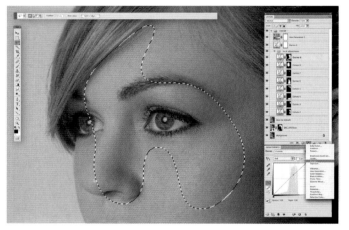

7 Local colour adjustments I like to make my skin tones fairly even in colour, saturation and tone. Create small shifts using the *Lasso Tool* with a large *Feather* (I use around 150px). Circle the area that needs to be adjusted and add a New Adjustment Layer. I prefer adjusting the individual Channels by a notch or two with a *Curves* adjustment layer. Refine the adjustment to prevent it affecting nearby areas using the attached Layer Mask.

8 Highlights Create a new layer set to the default *Normal* blending mode and select the *Brush Tool*, set it to ultra-soft and *White* at 100% *Opacity*/1% *Flow*. Extend and strengthen highlights that are already visible, and with practice you'll be able to create highlights that might be there if another light was added or the subject was shifted slightly. This step will be significantly easier if you use a graphics tablet and a stylus.

9 Carving In a new layer set to *Overlay* blending mode, 'paint' with an ultra-soft brush at 100% *Opacity*/1% *Flow*. Painting with white will create further highlights and painting with black will create further shading. Brush over the highlights you amplified in the previous step. You can also brush over highlights in the hair and clothing. Switch to black to create extra dimension and depth to the clothing, subject and overall image.

10 Resample the whites Create a new blank layer and make sure your *Foreground Color* is *White*. Go to *Select>Color Range* and adjust the *Fuzziness* slider until the selection represents a light dusting of highlights on the subject, and hit *OK*. Fill this selection with white (*command+delete*) then deselect (*command+d*). Mask away any areas that have created too heavy of a highlight for your liking.

Picture perfect
Every image will demand
different treatment, but these
steps should help put you on the
road to flawless results.

PORTRAIT KIT

FIND OUT ABOUT THE EQUIPMENT YOU NEED TO GET THE BEST SHOTS OF YOUR MOST ACCESSIBLE SUBJECT – FRIENDS AND FAMILY – WITH THIS COMPREHENSIVE GEAR GUIDE FOR PORTRAITS

CONTEMPORARY PORTRAITURE has moved on from the days of sitting in front of a mottled brown background in a stuffy studio and smiling politely for the camera. Nowadays, portraits need to exude fun, energy, laughter and capture something of the subject's character.

This new style of portraiture has become known as 'lifestyle' photography – but what exactly is it? Put simply, it's a portrait of a person living their life and doing the things they love. There's a massive market for this style of photography, so whether you just want to capture some great shots of the kids to put up on your wall, or you have more ambitious plans to earn some cash from portraiture, there are plenty of willing subjects around. What's more, you don't need to hire a studio and know how to operate studioflash – it's much better to get out and about, visit your subjects at home or shoot them in a location that's personal to them. This brings its own photographic challenges, however, and without the right gear you run the risk of your portraits turning out like a snapshot.

So, in the first section of this gear guide we walk you through the equipment you need to surmount the challenges location portraiture presents. As well as cameras themselves, we'll look at the best lenses for portraiture and which ones will help you take pictures that stand out from the crowd. You'll also need some lighting to give your shots the wow factor no matter what the weather, but don't panic if you're daunted by flash: we've picked out flashguns that aren't complicated to use. For the more confident photographers, we'll show you the advanced off-camera flash systems top lifestyle photographers use and there's advice on accessories and gadget bags, not forgetting the props, too! So, what are you waiting for? Dive in and start finding out about the gear you need to shoot cracking portraits.

Key contacts

Arctic Butterfly
www.visibledust.com

Canon
www.canon.co.uk

Cokin
www.intro2020.com

Gitzo
www.gitzo.co.uk

Giottos
www.daymen.co.uk

Green Clean
www.flaghead.co.uk

Hahnel
www.hahnel.ie

Hitech
www.formatt.co.uk

Hoodman
www.newprouk.co.uk

Jessops
www.jessops.com

Lowepro
www.daymen.co.uk

Kenko
www.intro2020.com

LaCie
www.lacie.com

Lastolite
www.lastolite.com

Lexar
www.lexar.com

Lowepro
www.lexar.com

Manfrotto
www.manfrotto.co.uk

Nikon
www.nikon.co.uk

Op/Tech
www.newprouk.co.uk

Peak Design
www.peakdesignltd.com

Rogue
www.daymen.co.uk

Samsung
www.samsung.co.uk

SanDisk
www.sandisk.co.uk

Sigma
www.sigma-imaging-uk.com

Slik
www.intro2020.com

Tamrac
www.intro2020.com

Tamron
www.intro2020.com

Velbon
www.intro2020.com

The novice lifestyle portrait photographer

When starting out, an entry-level camera, affordable lenses, a simple flash and a few accessories are all you need as you begin to shape your craft. There's really no need to rush out and spend a fortune at this stage – better to find your feet and make sure it's the style of photography you intend to pursue before making a serious investment. So, if you're buying your first 'proper' camera kit, take a look at our suggestions below...

Flash modifier

Flashguns at this end of the market don't offer manual control to reduce the flash power, so accessories to modify and diffuse the flash can really help. The £7 Jessops Universal Flash Diffuser simply slips over your flashgun to diffuse the light, or for more creative effects, such as a spotlight, Rogue offers three sizes of its Flashbender accessory, ranging from £24-£30.

Basic flashgun

Your camera's pop-up flash produces a burst of light that's too harsh for portraits, making images look more like a quick snap. But if you use a dedicated flashgun attached to the hotshoe, you can direct the flash away from your subject for a more subtle effect. They also boast more power than your pop-up unit, so when your subject is a bit further away, you'll still be able to light them properly. Look out for flashguns with the swivel and bounce facility, as well as TTL metering, such as the £80 Jessops 360AFD or £70 Metz 24 AF-1.

Entry-level camera

You don't need a pro camera to take great lifestyle portraits; an entry-level DSLR or Compact System Camera (CSC) with a kit lens is fine to start off with. The advantage of CSCs is that they're smaller and easier to carry, so you're more likely to have it to hand to grab those candid portraits. The range of CSC lenses and other accessories is limited compared to DSLRs, however, so if you want more versatility and flexibility, the latter is the way to go. For a CSC, check out the Sony NEX-C3 with 18-55mm kit lens for £500 or the Panasonic Lumix GF3 with 14-42mm kit lens for the same price. If you decide to go the DSLR route then look out for the £450 Pentax K-r with 18-55mm lens, £380 Canon EOS 1100D with 18-55mm lens or the £450 Nikon D3100 with 18-55mm VR lens.

Fast standard prime

A standard prime is a very popular lens for portraits and for good reason. Taking account of the APS-C crop factor, the 50mm focal length converts to around 75mm, depending on the camera you use, which is a great focal length of portraits. These lenses also boast a 'fast' f/1.8 aperture, so you can easily throw the background out of focus. They're cheap, too. All the major manufacturers have an own-brand model for around £100, like the £90 Canon 50mm f/1.8 II or £110 Sony 50mm f/1.8 SAM.

Small gadget bag

As your portrait kit begins to expand, you'll need a solution for both transporting and keeping it safe at home. The £40 Lowepro Nova 140AW shoulder bag provides room for a DSLR, flash and 50mm standard prime, but if you're thinking of carrying a superzoom and reflector, too, then check out the larger £50 Jessops Trek2.

Belt clip

If you want to keep a second body within easy reach, clip it to your belt using a dedicated accessory. Peak Design's Capture Camera Clip has just been launched and fits over your belt. It features a quick release plate and sa tough aluminium body. Also available is the b-grip, which is larger belt-mounted camera holder.

Superzoom

If you're looking for an affordable and versatile second lens for portraits, a superzoom is a good option. With focal lengths ranging from wide-angle through to telephoto, you can shoot wide group shots and tighter head and shoulder portraits without having to change lens. Superzooms at this end of the market use a 'slow' variable aperture, however, making those creative shallow depth-of-field effects a bit of a challenge. Sigma offers an 18-200mm f/3.5–5.6 DC lens for £180 or, if you want more zoom, take a look at the £500 Tamron 18-270mm f/3.5-6.3 Di II VC LD.

5-in-1 reflector

Whether you're working with natural light or flash, a reflector is an essential part of any portrait photographer's kit. Reflecting light that initially missed your subject back onto their face helps fill in the darker shadows for a more balanced portrait. There's a vast range of reflectors available, but we'd recommend the 5-in-1 varieties that offer translucent, black, white, gold and silver surfaces for different effects. Interfit do a 32-inch 5-in-1 reflector for £40.

The enthusiast lifestyle portrait photographer

You're starting to shoot friends, colleagues and even people you don't know, so you need more sophisticated kit to improve results. You'll want 'fast' aperture lenses to isolate your subjects from a background, manual control of your flashgun for subtle lighting effects and gear to take your flash off camera. When you're shooting outdoors, you'll also need some filters to control bright light, not to mention a gadget bag to keep it all in.

Mid-range flashgun

As you get more confident with flash, a mid-range flashgun will help you experiment more. As well as TTL, they boast manual functions so you can reduce the power output for a more subtle effect when working close-up. They also boast wireless capabilities for taking your flashgun off-camera and placing it to the side or behind your model for more impressive lighting. Models like the £170 Canon Speedlite 320EXII, £250 Nikon Speedlight SB-700 or £180 Metz 50 AF-1 have a slave function, which means they can be triggered by a burst of flash from your camera's pop-up unit. You can also control the output of each flash source in your camera's menu system to achieve the desired effect.

Mid-range DSLR

As you start to take your portraiture more seriously, you'll no doubt consider upgrading your camera. Generally speaking, mid-range DSLRs offer improved build quality over their entry-level counterparts, so they're equipped to handle a bit more hammer. They also boast higher resolutions for sharper images using low ISO speeds and they boast advanced features like wireless flash control: although some entry-level cameras feature this now, too. If you've already started investing in lenses from one brand, you'll probably want to stick with that manufacturer when you upgrade your camera body, but if you've not committed yet, the latest £640 Canon EOS 600D or £650 Nikon D5100 should go straight to the top of your list.

Fast standard zoom

Kit lenses are fine when you're starting out, but their general build quality and optical construction leaves much to be desired. When you're looking for a step up in quality, fast standard zooms are the way to go. They only cover the same focal length as your kit lens, but the fixed f/2.8 aperture at 50mm is perfect for portraits on an APS-C sensor and you'll appreciate the smoother zoom action and metal lens mount. Own-brand options can be expensive, but there's a range of third-party ones, too, like the £350 Tamron 17-50mm f/2.8 VC or £360 Sigma 17-70mm f/2.8-4 OS. Be prepared for some extra weight to carry, however, as the improved build and extra glass in these lenses makes them much heavier than your kit lens.

Fast-access camera bag

Lifestyle portraits involve grabbing those split-second moments, so you need to work quickly. Therefore, when you want to change lenses or swap memory cards, having a bag quite literally at your side is a real bonus. The £95 Speed Freak is the mid-sized bag in Think Tank's Speed convertible range, and allows you very fast access and lots of storage. It's an alternative to using a belt with separate pouches, such as the Tamrac Modular System or Lowepro's Street & Field series, both from around £10-£15.

Very 'fast' standard prime

The f/1.4 aperture of these lenses lets in twice as much as a f/1.8 lens, which is great when shooting in low light. Not only that, but the maximum aperture allows you to throw most of the image out of focus, just keeping small details like the lips and eyes in focus. For a more regular portrait, though, stopping down the aperture to f/2.8 will provide cracking corner-to-corner sharpness. For around £300, Canon and Nikon have their own versions and third-party options include the £375 Sigma 50mm f/1.4 EX DG HSM or the £430 Tamron 60mm f/2 SP Di II, which, although not as 'fast', doubles up as a 1:1 macro lens, too.

Lighting stand, flash bracket and umbrella

Once you start taking your flashgun off-camera, a whole host of creative possibilities open up. One of the most basic and classic approaches is to place your flashgun at a 45° to your subject and use a shoot-through umbrella to soften the light. To do this, you'll not only need the umbrella itself, but also a flashgun bracket to attach your flashgun and umbrella to, as well as a stand so you can position it securely without having to hold it. Westcott do a collapsible umbrella flash kit that includes a stand, umbrella and flashgun bracket for £65.

Wireless flash triggers

Using a lighting stand and umbrella can have its problems if you're using your camera's pop-up unit to fire the flash. The sensor on the flashgun needs to receive the flash in order to fire and if you position the flashgun where your umbrella blocks the line of sight from your pop-up unit, the off-camera flash won't fire. This is where wireless radio triggers – which send a radio signal from your camera to your flashgun – come into play. With one transmitter connected to your camera's hotshoe and one receiver on the flashgun, you can place your flashgun out of direct line of sight and it'll still fire. Seculine's Twinlink T2D costs £100 and offers radio and infrared controls, while Hahnel's £60 Combi RF is also a great buy.

Reflector on stand kit

Unless you've an assistant or a willing volunteer to hand-hold your reflector in the right place, operating your camera at the same time can be a challenge. A good solution is the Interfit Flat Panel Reflector & Stand package for £90 that features a 35x75in reflector, making it suitable for close-up or full-length shots.

Grip Reflector

A reflector is an invaluable lighting aid, but can be difficult to position when you have no one around to hold it for you. The £64 Lastolite TriGrip gets around this problem by boasting a solid handle that you can grip with one handle while shooting with the other.

Wide-angle zoom lens

Its not a traditional portrait lens, as the distortion associated with wide-angles will stretch the proportions of your subject's face. That said, a wide-angle lens will give you another option in your armoury, allowing you to capture more of the surroundings and get shots others won't. They're also essential if you find yourself in a small or enclosed space where you can't get far enough back from your model. Again, own-brand options are available, or take a look at the highly recommended £500 Sigma 10-20mm f/3.5 EX or £545 Tokina AT-X DX 11-16mm f/2.8 Pro.

In the bag

Flash Gels
Coloured gels slotted over your flashgun can produce colourful and fun creative flash effects. Try the £19 Lumiquest FXtra Gel System.

Back-up Body
A second DSLR body means you can have a telezoom attached to one camera and fast prime or wide-angle on the other, giving you multiple options without the inconvenience of having to keep changing lens.

White Balance Aid
With most lifestyle portraits, you'll be mixing ambient and flash light sources, which makes it tricky for the camera to get the White Balance right. Shooting in Raw and taking a quick shot of a grey card at the start of the shoot will help make sure the White Balance can be quickly and easily corrected across all your shots later in software. Check out the £16 Lastolite 30cm Ezybalance Grey Card.

Lightmeter
These aren't essential and many digital photographers get by without one, but when you start using off-camera flash and manual controls, they can be useful for getting your exposures spot-on. The Sekonic Flashmate L-308S offers a digital display, incident and reflected readings and four different modes for £170.

Filters
Many filter effects can be achieved in Photoshop – however, some can't, and for these you'll need to use filters. Polarising filters are great for adding more punch to your shots when shooting portraits in bright conditions as they reduce lens flare, cut out reflections and help darken down the blues in the sky. Check the diameter of your lens to get the right size filter, but, for an example, the Jessops 72mm Circular Polarising Filter costs £54. ND grads also allow you to balance the exposure between a bright sky and darker foreground when taking wide-angle portraits. Screw-on ND filters are available, but a filter holder system gives you more flexibility as you can use it across all your lenses. The Cokin Z-Pro ND kit costs £150.

Tripod
A tripod is an unlikely bit of kit for a lifestyle portrait photographer as you'll usually need to change shooting position quickly as your subject, particularly younger ones, move around. There are lots of tripods available, including one that lets you shoot very low to the ground, but a good model to start with is the £50 Manfrotto 055PROXB. As an alternative, you might also want to look at monopods for flexibility.

Remote release
For a more relaxed or spontaneous moment, a remote release allows you to set a shot up and then move away from the camera to interact with the subject. Our favourite basic model is the £25 Hahnel RC280 Remote release.

The semi-pro lifestyle portrait photographer

Having cut your teeth in lifestyle portraiture, you now want to make some money doing it part-time. It's a competitive market, though, and with dozens of pros looking for the same customers, you need the best equipment to compete. The big question is whether you're going to upgrade to full-frame, with all the extra investment in new glass involved and you'll want to look at multiple flash set-ups and top-end reflectors, too.

Semi-pro DSLR

If you already own a suite of lenses designed for the smaller APS-C sensor, then it'll be a hard decision and large investment to upgrade to full-frame. If you stick to APS-C, but want the best available, then top-of-the-range models offer superb build and handling (making them more comfortable to use), more AF points, faster focusing and a faster continuous shooting. The £1,100 12.3-megapixel Nikon D300s performs well in low light, but if you're after more resolution and full HD video, check out the £1,200 Canon EOS 7D. The advantage of going full-frame is that the larger image sensor gives each pixel a little more space to breathe and improves the overall picture quality – particularly at high ISOs. The £1,850 12.1-megapixel Nikon D700 produces incredible results using ISO speeds up to ISO 3200, but if it's resolution and HD video you want, go for the £1,700 21-megapixel Canon EOS 5D Mk II.

Fast standard zoom

If you need new glass for a full frame camera, then you can thankfully forget about all that confusing crop-factor stuff. Fast standard zooms offer a versatile focal length from wide-angle to short telephoto, and that fixed f/2.8 maximum aperture is great for creating a shallow depth-of-field and isolating your subjects from the background. The full frame game is not cheap, though, and you'll need £1,000 to get hold of the Canon EF 24-70mm f/2.8L or £1,230 for the Nikon 24-70mm f/2.8.

'Fast' telephoto zoom

When you need to crop in tighter for a head and shoulders portrait, a fast telezoom is perfect. Pro lenses have a fixed f/2.8, so shallow depth-of-field isn't a problem, and the optics deliver incredibly sharp results. The most recent releases also feature image stabilisation (Canon IS or Nikon VR), which reduces camera shake when using longer focal lengths and slow shutter speeds. The Nikon 70-200mm f/2.8 ED VR II costs £1,635 or £1,050 for the Canon 70-200mm f/2.8L IS II USM. Also consider the capable but slower (and more affordable) £500 Canon EF 70-200mm f/4L USM.

Wide-angle zoom

In reality, the 24mm wide-angle focal length on your standard zoom should be wide enough for all but a very few portraits. That said, a wide-angle zoom will generally perform better at 24mm, giving less distortion or chromatic aberrations than your standard zoom, and you can go wider should you want to. The Nikon 16-35 f/4G ED costs £850, while the Canon 16-35mm f/2.8L II USM is £1,160.

Very 'fast' telephoto prime

The 85mm f/1.4 is the ideal portrait lens, flattering facial features while slightly compressing perspective to isolate your subjects from the background. They are incredibly sharp too, but expensive. The Sigma 85mm f/1.4EX DG is great value at £730, especially when you consider the Nikon 85mm f/1.4G is £1,265 and Canon 85mm f/1.2L II USM is £1,760.

Camera bag

With two or three larger lenses, filters, flash, radio triggers and other essentials like batteries and memory cards, that small gadget bag isn't going to cut the mustard. The £120 Lowepro Magnum 200AW is very large, has an all-weather covers and lots of dividers to keep your gear safe. If you're after a bag that doubles up as both a shoulder bag and a waist belt for quick access to your kit, then check out the £120 Think Tank Speed Freak v2.0.

Softbox kit

Softboxes are another method of diffusing flashlight – only until fairly recently have they been the preserve of the studio photographer. Smaller softboxes that attach to standard flashguns are now available, making them convenient on location. They offer an advantage over brollies, too, as the four sides of the softbox direct the light better, giving you more control over where it'll fall. You need to check the compatibility of any kit with your flashgun, but look at the £115 Westcott 70cm Apollo kit or £103 Lastolite 54cm Ezybox.

Wireless flash trigger

If you're planning on using multiple flash set-ups, look for wireless trigger sets that use additional receivers. The £90 Interfit Titan Pro system is superb value, while the most popular model with pros is the £269 PocketWizard Plus II Set.

Framed reflector

If you're shooting with some assistance, consider investing in a framed reflector, which is more sturdy and easier to handle than a traditional type. The best are by California Sunbounce, which makes them in four sizes and various effects. Prices start at around £1,110 for the 60x90cm Micro-mini reflector.

In the bag

Skylight Diffuser Panel
It might seem an odd statement, but when shooting lifestyle portraits on location, the sun can be a real pain. Not only will your models often squint, but the deep shadows and bright highlights make controlling your exposure a big challenge. You can always seek out some light shade, but that can also present problems with messy backgrounds or dappled light, so many pros use a large sunscreen instead. In effect, it's a large stretched piece of fabric in a frame and, using a pole or stand, it's positioned above your subject's head to cast a light shadow over them while you shoot. The £306 California Sunbounce Pro Sunswatter comes as a complete kit and is like a giant fly squatter, so you'll need an assistant to hold it. The Lastolite Skylight system can be free-standing using standard light stands. There's no kit available, though, so you'll need to buy the fabric, frame and two grip heads separately, which will set you back around £255.

Second flashgun
Creative lifestyle portraits are often produced using several light sources. You might like to invest in a second flashgun so that you can light your subjects from the side and back at the same time for an attractive rim light or hairlight effect. Top-end models also kick out more power (look out for Flash Guide Numbers: the higher the number, the greater the power), which is important when using umbrellas or softboxes as they reduce the amount of flashlight reaching your subject. Try Nikon or Canon models: £320 for the Nikon Speedlight SB-900 or £370 for the Canon Speedlite 580EX II. Remember you may need a wireless trigger too.

Post-production

The gear you'll need for top-end lifestyle portraits isn't just the hardware. Just take a look at your local portrait studio's website and you'll see the funky colour splash, cross-process or high-saturation effects that can only be achieved using software.

Image enhancement
For general image organisation and enhancement, including good basic portrait retouching tools like Red Eye Removal and Teeth Whitening, Photoshop Elements 10 at £80 will suffice for the novice or enthusiast portrait photographer.

Image management
If you start taking on a lot of commissions, shoot Raw and need to turn shots around quickly or upload easily to bespoke web galleries, the advanced features and functionality of packages like Adobe's £218 Lightroom 3 or Apple's £140 Aperture 3 are worth their weight in gold.

Advanced retouching
Pro portrait lenses like 85mm f/1.4 are so sharp, they're pretty unforgiving and will show up spots and blemishes, even on the smoothest of complexions. For advanced and quick retouching, Portrait Professional offers a whole series of adjustments, including removing blemishes, lighting eyes, adjusting hair tone and even reshaping facial features, all automatically. It's better suited for classic head and shoulder portraits than family or group portraiture, but as it's now available for just £30, it's a bit of a steal.

Creative effects
With Photoshop Elements loaded, a whole host of creative effects are available if you have the skill and time. If not, OnOne's £325 Plug In Suite 5 offers a range of effects at the touch of a button. There are five plug-ins in all, but look out for PhotoTools 2.6 for creative effects, PhotoFrame 4.6 for adding digital frames around your shots and PhotoTune 3 for optimising the dynamic range or correcting the colour in your lifestyle portraits.

Printers
With your lifestyle portraits shot, organised and enhanced, the final and often most rewarding stage is sharing your work with family, friends or clients. Digital distribution has its place and reaches lots of people quickly, but there's nothing better than a framed print on the wall to enjoy day after day. Affordable A3+ is the way to go, so consider the £285 Epson Stylus Photo R1400 or £170 Canon PIXMA IX6550. It's the next best thing to having a printing company produce your professional prints.

Accessory belts and pouches

If you do shoot portraits on location with a lot of pro kit, you're either going to have a very heavy bag on your shoulder or a rucksack that spreads the weight. Either way it's difficult to get to your gear quickly. Another solution, however, is a belt that allows you to carry cameras, lenses and accessories around your waist for easy access. They're usually modular systems, so you can configure the number and size of the pouches attached to the belt to suit your kit. The Lowepro S+F Deluxe Technical belt costs £40, but remember to budget extra for the pouches you need, or the £70 Lowepro Outback 200 beltpack includes pouches for one camera with lens attached and two extra lenses to boot.

Portable studioflash kit

If you're serious about flash, invest in a studioflash kit. Cheap entry-level kits are available for a few hundred pounds, but they require mains power, which isn't always available on location and they're pretty cumbersome, too. A portable kit gives you the same amount of power using a battery pack, so you could shoot a lifestyle portrait on top of Mount Snowdon if you wanted, and they come in smaller cases, making them easier to carry. The £1,549 Elinchrom Ranger Quadra RX 2 Head kit is the popular choice with pros, while the £780 Lencarta Safari Classic Battery & 2 Heads kit is great value.

The best lenses for portraits

The standard kit zoom supplied with your camera is a good general purpose lens for shooting satisfactory portraits, but we'd recommend you consider one of these two types of optics for far better quality results

The 'standard' 50mm f/1.8

IN THE DAYS OF 35MM film SLRs, you'd invariably find a 50mm f/1.8 prime lens attached to the front of almost every SLR, and it remained popular until the late eighties. It was around this time that standard zooms started to appear. With their variable focal lengths ranging from wide-angle to short-telephoto, the 28-70mm (and similar) lens represented a step forward in terms of flexibility and sadly it led to the demise of the 50mm as the standard lens of choice. However, its popularity has recently seen a resurgence for a number of reasons.

The first is that it's a very inexpensive lens to get hold of. With 50mm lenses from the likes of Canon, Nikon and Sony costing just over £100 new, and used versions available for a little over half that, they're an affordable choice for most of us. To add further credence to the value-for-money argument, consider this fact. The lens of choice for many portrait pros has long been the 85mm telephoto, which for an f/1.8 version will set you back around £300. If your DSLR uses an APS-C sensor, as most do, a 50mm that costs you £100 equates to a 75mm f/1.8 (or 80mm f/1.8 if you use Canon) – but with an effective saving of around £200!

Also, if you don't mind buying a used manual focus lens, you can pick one up for around £25. So for the price of a decent memory card, you can get a high-quality piece of glass that may be a few decades old and lack AF, but won't leave you wanting in the optical department. So, there's no denying a 50mm lens is affordable, but what else does it

offer? Well, the biggest selling point must surely be its maximum aperture of f/1.8. Having a lens with such a fast maximum aperture offers stacks of potential. With your average 18-55mm having a maximum aperture of f/3.5-5.6, the 50mm is two to three stops faster, giving a brighter viewfinder image and allowing you to shoot handheld in low light, while using lower ISO ratings than you would normally get away with.

The most remarkable benefit of the wide maximum aperture is the extremely shallow depth-of-field when you shoot wide open, which helps isolate the main subject from its surroundings. This single feature provides significant creative opportunities, especially in the field of portraiture. The 50mm lens also scores better than virtually any other lens in the size and weight department. Weighing around 150 grams and measuring about 5cm in length, it's the perfect optic to keep with you, especially when you're travelling and when storage is at a premium.

The final benefit is possibly the most important – image quality. As with the majority of prime lenses, the optical quality from the humble 50mm lens is arguably better than all but the high-end zooms and in terms of sharpness, is superior to a standard zoom. In terms of sharpness, distortion, light fall-off and contrast and even when used wide open, you'll have little to complain about. So, there you have it, a small, lightweight and affordable lens with a super-fast aperture and razor-sharp optics. Is it not time you bought one?

AF 50mm f/1.8 lenses

You'll find that brands with full-frame DSLRs in their range have retained 50mm lenses in their line-up. If you're on a budget, avoid the faster f/1.4 and f/1.2 variants aimed at pros, as they're larger and cost far more. The Canon and Nikon lenses have been around for years, so look for mint-condition used lenses!

Canon EF 50mm f/1.8II
Guide Price: £130
Street Price: £100
Dimensions (WxL): 68.2x41mm
Weight: 130g
The Mk II lens is virtually identical to the original – both are well worth buying.

Nikon 50mm f/1.8D
Guide Price: £135
Street Price: £110
Dimensions (WxL): 63x39mm
Weight: 160g
Small, light and very sharp. Look for the 'D' tag to avoid buying an older series lens.

Sony DT 50mm f/1.8 SAm
Guide Price: £160
Street Price: £150
Dimensions (WxL): 70x45mm
Weight: 170g
A great lens but not so easy to find. Remember, Minolta Dynax lenses fit too!

What's the big deal about the 50mm's f/1.8 aperture?

You have to experience a lens as fast as the 50mm to really understand and appreciate its benefits but, trust us, once you've tried you'll be hooked. The 50mm's f/1.8 aperture enables you to throw the background completely out of focus and isolate the main subject from its setting. This set of images shows the changes in depth-of-field at various apertures from f/1.8 to f/22.

Telephoto zooms

IN THE LATTER YEARS of the film era, the 70-300mm was the most popular choice of telezoom due to the versatility of its focal lengths. For most digital SLR users, the 55-200mm covers a similar zoom range, thanks to the 1.5x effective increase in focal length associated with the smaller sensor size. That's great news, as a 55-200mm lens is smaller and lighter than a 70-300mm lens and its also far more affordable.

The 55-200mm zoom is suitable for a wide variety of subjects. At its widest end, it's perfect for general portraiture, while zooming to the telephoto end is ideal if your subject is further away or you are shooting candids. There is a wide number of 55-200mm zooms available and all perform well and produce decent results. We've offered you a closer look at the Nikon and Tamron models as we feel that they offer

particularly good value for money. Most 55-200mm lenses are budget zooms, offering good enough quality for general purpose photography, but if you're intending to produce large prints, you should look at upgrading to a mid-range zoom with a faster maximum aperture and better optics. For this reason, we've included Canon's 70-200mm f/4L USM as its one of the best in its class.

You may find stores try selling you a 70-300mm, which effectively behaves as a 105-450mm. While a great choice for digital SLRs with a full-frame sensor, we'd not recommend the 70-300mm for use with cameras using the APS-C sensor due to problems associated with the increased focal length, such as camera shake and its restrictive angle-of-view at close range.

Canon EF 70-200mm f/4L USM

Guide Price: £790
Street Price: £550
www.canon.co.uk
Lens optics: 16 elements in 13 groups
Lens mount: Metal
Maximum aperture: f/4
Minimum aperture: f/32
Minimum focus: 1.2m
Filter thread: 67mm
Weight: 705g
Supplied accessories: None
Dimensions: 76x172mm
Compatibility: All Canon EOS models

Canon has a number of budget zooms and also a couple of pro-spec f/2.8 options. This is one of two mid-range f/4 lenses (the other offers an image stabiliser) and arguably the best value of Canon's four 70-200mm zooms. It boasts an f/4 maximum aperture throughout its focal length range and these faster optics result in it being a longer and heavier lens than budget alternatives. However, this drawback is soon forgotten once you start using it – the autofocus is whisper-quiet and very accurate, while the image quality is far superior compared to cheaper zooms, with less distortion, a lot more detail and better contrast. Unless you're a pro requiring the f/2.8 maximum aperture, this lens (or the more expensive IS version) is good enough for all your needs. Well worth checking out.

Verdict
It costs far more than budget zooms but optical quality is far superior and worth the extra.

Handling	★★★★★
Features	★★★★★
Autofocus	★★★★★
Image quality	★★★★★
Value for money	★★★★☆
OVERALL	★★★★★

Nikon AF-S VR DX 55-200mm f/4-5.6G ED

Guide Price: £320
Street Price: £210
www.nikon.co.uk
Lens Optics: 15 elements in 11 groups
Lens mount: Plastic
Maximum aperture: f/4-5.6
Minimum aperture: f/22-32
Minimum focus: 1.1m
Filter thread: 52mm
Weight: 335g
Supplied accessories: Case and hood
Dimensions: 73x99.5mm
Compatibility: APS-C Nikon

This version sits alongside the original Nikon DX 55-200mm G ED Nikkor lens but boasts a VR (Vibration Reduction) facility. The result is a slight increase in the size and weight but more importantly improved performance in low light and at the telephoto end due to shake being minimised. The Nikon boasts a very wide zoom ring but the slim manual focusing ring at the end of the barrel could do with more width. The autofocus is quick, quiet and responsive even in low light and is one of the better lenses in terms of sharpness. As with other zooms of this type, images at the wide to mid-focal lengths are better than at 200mm. At its maximum aperture sharpness is satisfactory, and improves significantly as soon as the lens is stopped down, proving best at f/8-13.

Verdict
A great telezoom thanks to decent all-round performance and the VR facility.

Handling	★★★★☆
Features	★★★★☆
Autofocus	★★★★☆
Image quality	★★★★☆
Value for money	★★★★☆
OVERALL	★★★★☆

Tamron AF 55-200mm f/4-5.6 LD Di II

Guide Price: £160
Street Price: £120
www.intro2020.co.uk
Lens Optics: 13 elements in nine groups
Lens mount: Plastic
Maximum aperture: f/4-5.6
Minimum aperture: f/32
Minimum focus: 0.95m
Filter thread: 52mm
Weight: 300g
Supplied accessories: Hood
Dimensions: 71.6x83mm
Compatibility: APS-C (various fittings)

This zoom has proven extremely popular thanks to a combination of low price, decent build quality and good all-round performance. The wide zoom ring is very easy to grip and has a smooth action, but as with the Nikon, the manual focusing ring is thin and not the easiest to use. The autofocus turns in a good performance – it's not the quickest or quietest but it is accurate and performs better than expected in low light. As with most 55-200mm zooms, it performs best at the shorter end but quality through the range is good, especially once the aperture is stopped down, with f/8-11 giving the sharpest results. Please note this lens is designed for use with APS-C sensors only and isn't compatible with larger sensor sizes. It is available in Canon, Nikon and Sony fittings.

Verdict
A budget zoom lens that turns in a better performance than you expect for the price.

Handling	★★★★☆
Features	★★★★☆
Autofocus	★★★☆☆
Image quality	★★★★☆
Value for money	★★★★☆
OVERALL	★★★★☆

Top picks: Flashguns and studioflash kits

Photography is simply the manipulation of light. But, sometimes, natural light doesn't provide the effect you want, so we've selected our top flashguns and studio kits to help shed light on products that offer great value

Nissin Speedlite Di622 II

www.kenro.co.uk; 01793 615836

MAIN SPECIFICATIONS

Guide Price: £150
Street Price: £130
Guide Number: 44-62 (ISO 100, m)
Flash coverage: 16-70mm (24-105mm)
Recycling time: four to six seconds
Bounce facility: Yes (0 to 90°)
Swivel facility: Yes (0 to 270°)
TTL: Yes
AF assist beam: Yes
Strobe flash: No
Wireless flash: Yes

The Nissin Di622 has excellent build quality for a flash unit costing under £150; it's as good as models costing twice its price. This flashgun also has some rewarding features that set it apart from many other flashguns at this price range. These include second-curtain sync, slave flash and a standby mode that kicks in after two minutes of non-use to save your battery power. It also includes a flash stand, a diffuser for coverage as wide as 16mm and a fill-in reflector. There is no LCD panel on the rear; instead, a series of LEDs indicate power and a single button handles the modes. The Nissin Di622 MkII flashgun is available for Canon, Nikon and Sony DSLRs and considering the quality of features and the reasonable price, offers a decent cut-price alternative to branded models.

Sigma EF-530 DG Super

www.sigma-imaging-uk.com; 01707 329999

MAIN SPECIFICATIONS

Guide Price: £250
Street Price: £150
Guide Number: 28-53 (ISO 100, m)
Flash coverage: 16-70mm (24-105mm)
Recycling time: four to six seconds
Bounce facility: Yes (0-90°)
Swivel facility: Yes (0-270°)
TTL: Yes
AF assist beam: Yes
Strobe flash: Yes
Wireless flash: Yes

Sigma not only makes great value lenses, it also boasts a couple of excellent flashguns, with this being its top model. The EF-530 is available in Canon, Nikon, Pentax, Sigma and Sony versions, and is packed with stacks of features. In fact, it will take you quite a while to read the EF-530's instruction manual to get to grips with them all! One interesting feature is the High Speed Sync, which allows you to fire the unit at shutter speeds above your camera's usual flash sync speed. The unit can also be used as a master or a slave unit, and offers a wide-angle flash diffuser panel. The unit is also easy to use with the buttons spaced out, and a bright and clear LCD monitor. The battery compartment slider, however, could be a potential weak spot after sustained use. An excellent flashgun.

Interfit EX150 MK II outfit

www.interfitphotographic.com

MAIN SPECIFICATIONS

Guide Price: £250
Street Price: £220
No. of heads: 2x 150Ws
Power: 19-150Ws
Guide number (ISO 100, m): 22
Modelling lamp: Full (100W)/Off
Fitting: EX type
Trigger Voltage: 5v

KIT INCLUDES
2x flash heads, 2x stands, 2x sync leads,
2x power leads, 1x white brolly,
2x spill kills, 1x softbox, 1x DVD

Replacing the successful EX150 kit, the Mk II version has some impressive new features. The heads are a decent size, with a strong polycarbonate build, and are compatible with the full Interfit range of accessories. Though there is no storage bag with this kit, the box it comes in is sturdy and adequate for holding it. The modelling lamps give a useful amount of light and the flash power (1/8 to full-power) is very respectable and, when channelled by the spill kills, can add 50% to the Guide Number. Light temperature is a little on the cool side, so using Raw or a manual WB setting is advised. This is a great kit for the money and a good choice for the amateur. It may not be as extensive as some, but the build quality of the equipment more than makes up for it.

Elinchrom D-Lite 4 IT outfit

www.flashcentre.com; 0207 8375649

MAIN SPECIFICATIONS

Guide Price: £730
Street Price: £550
No. of heads: 2x 400Ws
Power: 25-400Ws
Modelling lamp: Full (100W)/
proportional/Low/Off
Fitting: EX type
Trigger Voltage: 5v

STUDIO 2 GO OUTFIT INCLUDES
2x flash heads, 2x stands, 2x power leads,
2x softbox (one medium, one small),
1x light bag, 1x stand bag

This update of the original D-Lite is one of the best kits for beginners. The heads are compact but sturdy, and feature an integral Skyport wireless trigger. The heads are available in 200 and 400-Watt versions (D-Lite 2 IT & D-Lite 4 IT respectively) and if possible, we recommend you buy the 400-Watt heads as the extra power is very useful. The control panel couldn't be easier to use. An LED shows the current power setting with two large buttons beneath allowing it to be changed. Other controls allow you to set the modelling light to be on at minimum or full power, off, or proportional to the power setting, which is set in 1/10th increments. There is also a button to switch the audible ready 'beep' on or off. The D-Lite kit has everything you need to get started.

Ringflash adaptors

We test two 'budget' adaptors designed to mimic the flattering and funky effect produced by a ringflash

MANY PROFESSIONAL fashion and portrait photographers love using a ringflash to capture images with a distinctive shadowless lighting effect. With a basic ringflash kit costing several hundred pounds, a number of manufacturers have produced adaptors that, when fitted over the head of a standard flashgun, aim to mimic a ringflash effect. We test the two most popular models from Orbis and RayFlash.

Orbis

The Orbis is made from tough ABS plastic, which is able to withstand heavy general usage and seems durable enough to survive a drop, although we've not tested that fact! At 20cm diameter, the ring area is larger than the RayFlash (although the 86mm tunnel for the lens is smaller), and at 500 grams, it's also slightly heavier. The standard way to use the Orbis is to slip the flashgun into the housing and hand-hold the flash with your left hand, resting your thumb and forefinger on the grooved surface on the Orbis. The housing has a flexible grip that holds a variety of flash heads, so if you've a well-known brand of flash, it will most likely fit. With the lens poking through the tunnel, the set-up works well, but does become uncomfortable if you're shooting for a prolonged period of time. In this instance, we'd recommend the optional Orbis arm, an adjustable aluminium bracket that fixes to the flashgun's hotshoe and the camera's tripod bush. The £50 arm was unavailable for this test, but you should consider it if you plan to use the Orbis for extended periods of time.

The output from the flash travels straight up and around the ring, which has a diffuser around the entire front surface. Within the Orbis ring, the light is distributed to provide an even effect and to limit light loss.

Because the flashgun is handheld, flash exposures aren't straightforward. You can use Canon's infrared flash trigger or Nikon's CLS flash system for TTL flash, or independent dedicated off-camera cords. This has the advantage of providing more accurate flash exposures. If you use a third-party flash trigger, such as a Pocket Wizard, Hahnel Combi RF or Seculine TwinLink (used for this test), TTL flash information isn't communicated to the camera, so you need to set your flash to manual power settings. This involves taking test shots at ½ power, ¼ power etc and adjusting power until you have a decent exposure. It's also worth noting that because it's hand-held, you can position the Orbis to shoot from an angle, much as you would a softbox or beauty light.

It took a fair bit of effort to fit our Canon Speedlite 580EX II into the Orbis housing, but once in, the grip was tight and secure. Our Canon 28-70mm f/2.8 lens fitted snugly through the tunnel, but occasionally we found the AF/M switch had been moved to manual by contact with the Orbis tunnel, so do ensure you keep an eye on this.

The output from the Orbis was excellent and it allows enough flash output through to illuminate subjects a few feet away.

Catchlights
The Orbis delivers a prominent catchlight and even spread of light.

Price: £200 (Guide)/ £185 (Street)	
Supplied accessories: Case, strap, self-adhesive pad	
WEBSITE: www.orbisflash.com	

Orbis users should buy the £50 Orbis Arm for better handling. It can be tripod-mounted too.

Verdict

Having to hand-hold the Orbis means it's more of an effort to use than the RayFlash, but it is versatile as you can position it at any angle. But we'd suggest you buy the optional arm to improve handling. Ideally, use a dedicated off-camera lead for TTL compatibility, but even if using manual flash, you should be able to produce flattering portraits.

 Like Well made, beautiful lighting effect, near-universal compatibility

 Dislike Hand-held without optional arm. No TTL flash without dedicated accessories

HIGHLY RATED ★★★★☆

OVERALL ★★★★☆

RayFlash

The RayFlash is a less chunky and lighter unit than the Orbis but just as well made, and has a considerably different design. The ringflash diffuser is smaller and thinner, although the tunnel through which the lens sits is wider. The RayFlash is designed to be used with the flashgun mounted on the hotshoe. Because it's so light, the flashgun's head supports its weight, so there's little undue pressure on the hotshoe. The end that attaches to the flashgun is angled so that the flashgun's head faces forward when fitted. This has the advantage of the ringflash adaptor being positioned securely around the lens and, unlike the Orbis, negates the need for the photographer to hand-hold the unit. The other major benefit is that because the flashgun sits on the hotshoe, it retains TTL flash functions, meaning you don't have to invest in an off-camera cord or worry about having to calculate the exposure. These two factors means that the RayFlash handles better than the Orbis, but more importantly for beginners is far easier to use. It's also worth noting that you have the option of fitting a remote trigger/off-camera lead to the RayFlash and use the flashgun away from the camera much as you can with the Orbis.

When fired, the flash output travels through a series of prisms and reflectors that, like the Orbis, aims to distribute the light evenly around the ring. The output from the flash travels up and around the ring, which has a diffuser around the entire front surface. Within the RayFlash ring, the light is distributed to provide an even effect and to limit light loss. Where flashgun's head fits is smaller than the Orbis' and designed to fit particular models of flashgun. Therefore, you need to buy the correct RayFlash model for your flashgun, which is easy to do by referring to the table on the distributor's website: www.flaghead.co.uk.

The adaptor's flash housing has a locking pin that holds the flashhead securely, but take care when tightening it as our sample cracked a little when we twisted it too far. Once the RayFlash is fitted, you can start taking pictures straight away with the comfort of knowing that the camera is taking care of the exposures. You should, however, regularly check the LCD monitor to ensure images are not over or underexposed. If you're not happy with the results, you can boost or reduce power using flash exposure compensation.

The RayFlash is easier to use than the Orbis thanks to it retaining TTL. However, you do need to keep an eye on exposures as getting too close will lead to overexposure. While the RayFlash is efficient, don't stray more than a couple of metres from your subject as you'll quickly lose its effect. Its output is very similar to that created by the Orbis.

Top tips for using adaptors

- Zoom the flashgun's head to its maximum setting to help increase the flash's range
- Regularly review images and the histogram to ensure good exposures, in particular when you have moved closer or further away from the subject
- Fit a colour gel to your flashgun's head if you want to change the colour temperature of the flash output
- Write down your exposure settings for later reference

Fun flash
The RayFlash is very easy to use and delivers great results.

Price: £170 (Guide)/ £160 (Street)
Supplied accessories: Case, strap, self-adhesive pad
Website: www.flaghead.co.uk

Verdict

The design of the RayFlash gives it a couple of distinct advantages over the Orbis. Its lighter weight means it is easier to use and the advantage of TTL flash will prove a major benefit to those inexperienced with flash photography or wanting to work quickly. For these reasons, the RayFlash is a better overall choice to the Orbis.

Like Nice design, retains TTL functions, nice effect

Dislike Design of holding clamp; not as universal as Orbis

OVERALL ★★★★★

Test conclusion

We were a little sceptical about ringflash adapters before this test. Can a piece of plastic with a ring-shaped diffuser really match the performance of a proper 'pro' ringflash? Well, we found they can't, but they do a very good job nonetheless at getting close to replicating the effect. Sure, neither can match a true ringflash, but they do come close in some respects, delivering an effect that is sure to suit those who can't afford the high price of a ringflash but wish to capture images that reproduce its lighting effect. There is little doubt that a ringflash is easier and more enjoyable to use, but let's be honest, it's an accessory very few of us can afford to buy, especially as it's something that won't be used on a regular basis. The Orbis and RayFlash both offer a very good buy for those looking to add a modern, funky fashion feel to their portraits. Both deliver great results, but the RayFlash is the better buy thanks to its neater design, which offers TTL flash photography without the need for a dedicated off-camera lead.

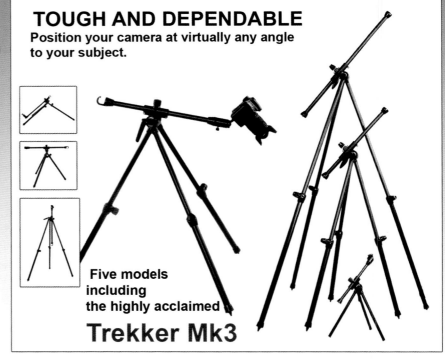

Buyers' Guide: Lighting aids

Whether working with ambient light or shooting in a studio with flash, reflectors and diffusers are an inexpensive and versatile aid to help manipulate light. We show you the main types to consider

THERE IS A COMMON misconception that you need expensive equipment to get professional-looking portraits. While a better camera and superior optics do make a difference, there are many affordable bits of kit that can lead to far better pictures if used correctly. Lighting aids – in other words, reflectors and diffusers – are two such items, proving useful whether you're using daylight, studioflash or any other form of lighting.

The various technique articles featured earlier in this guide provide some perfect examples of how and when to use lighting aids

with daylight, but it's worth remembering that they're also suitable for use with any subject that requires lighting control, so are great for still-lifes or close-ups. And, of course, they can be used in the studio, too: a reflector, for instance, is often used to bounce light from the key light source to fill in shadows on the subject, negating the need for a second flash head.

There are several different types of lighting aids available in different sizes, shapes and colours, from small hand-held options to those that require a stand or assistant to hold them. For the majority of amateurs and enthusiasts, a

small hand-held option is suitable for most needs, while for the more avid photographers who like to dabble in money-making photography, larger reflectors and diffusers prove far more effective, especially when shooting on location.

Our Buyers' Guide covers a range of products from all the popular brands that are worth considering for everyday use, but check their websites for more specialist products, too. We've also a comparison test of a number of 5-in-1 reflector kits, which will help you make the right choice and save you money, too.

Reflector size guide	
30cm	12in
50cm	20in
56cm	22in
81cm	32in
95cm	37in
107cm	42in
120cm	47in
70x110cm	28x44in
90x120cm	36x48in
100x165cm	40x66in
60x90cm	24x36in
90x125cm	36x50in
100x150cm	39x59in
130x190cm	52x76in
180x245cm	72x98in

California Sunbounce

www.theflashcentre.com

The California Sunbounce range of reflectors is a favourite with professionals thanks to their stability, build quality and light weight. The reflector panels are fitted to aluminium frames that come in various sizes and are quick and easy to assemble, disassemble and pack up for storage and transportation. There is a good choice of reflective panels available, although not every colour is suitable for every frame, but you still have several options open to you (the downloadable PDF catalogue has a very useful easy-reference table).

While you can buy extra panels to use with a frame, the difference in price for complete kits and individual panels isn't that wide, so it's often worth buying the complete outfit to save you having to swap panels while on location. As with other brands, there are silver/white and gold/white reflector options, but you'll find that there are other reflective finishes eg zebra/white (zebra is a mix of gold and silver), as well as a number of translucent diffuser options too.

As they're made for professional use, you'll find that they're relatively expensive, but they are made to last for years of professional use and are produced from the

best possible materials. The Sunbounce system is extensive, so contact importers The Flash Centre if you require further details, or download the catalogue at: www.sunbounce.com.

Because the number of options is huge, we've listed the different reflector ranges below and stated the price of the two most popular reflective colours. While a number of sizes are available, we'd recommend the Mini or Pro as your first choice, and the Mega (stated as Big in the catalogue) if you're a very keen enthusiast. Here are the main options:

Micro-mini: (60x90cm)
Silver/white: **£101**; Zebra/white: **£125**
Mini: (90x125cm)
Silver/white: **£156**; Zebra/white: **£190**
Pro: (130x190cm)
Silver/white: **£235**; Zebra/white: **£275**
Big: (180x245cm)
Silver/white: **£370**; Zebra/white: **£430**

While a couple of translucent panels are available for the Pro and Mega panels, for diffusing purposes we'd recommend you check out the Sun Swatter. This is a large diffuser that is ideal for outdoor use as it can be held by a boon over the subject and outside of the image area. It's easy to assemble and designed to be used in windy conditions. There are two sizes available and a number of options for the light-reducing value of the translucent material ($1/3$, $2/3$ or one-stop light diffusion). We'd recommend the smaller Sun Swatter with the $1/3$ or $2/3$-stop diffuser as a good first option.

Other specialist reflectors in the range include the Sun-Mover, which allows for additional control of the spread of light and the Sun Cage – a purpose-made mobile studio for location shooting.
Sun Swatter (130x190cm)
$1/3$ stop complete **£230**
Sun Swatter (130x190cm)
$2/3$ Stop complete **£240**
Sun Swatter Giant (180x245cm)
$1/3$ stop complete **£385**
Sun Swatter Giant (180x245cm)
$2/3$ Stop Complete **£400**

Kenro

www.kenro.co.uk

Kenro produces a circular and a rectangular 5-in-1 kit. The circular reflectors measure 12in, 22in, 32in and 42in, and cost £16, £30, £55 and £68 respectively. The rectangular kits measure 28x44in, 36x48in and 40x66in, and cost £56, £75 and £99 respectively. All the kits are supplied in a bag with a translucent panel and a reversible gold, silver, white and black cover.

Kenro also offers a range of reflectors and diffusers with handles called Easy Grips. It has three 60x90cm (24x36in) models in the

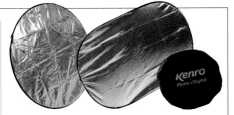

range: the £41 translucent and the £45 silver/white and sunlight/white variants. Each 5-in-1 reflector kit features a translucent panel over which a reversible gold, silver, white or black cover can be attached. It folds down into a handy round zip bag when not in use.

Calumet

www.calumetphoto.co.uk

Calumet is a major photo retailer and has an extensive number of own-brand photo accessories, including its ZipDisc range of collapsible reflectors. These include two colour reflectors, translucent panels and four-colour sleeves (gold/silver/white/black). The ZipDisc kits are as follows:

● **Translucent white ZipDisc panel**
The circular diffuser at the heart of its 5-in-1 kit is available on its own, too.
56cm £15; 81cm £26;
107cm £37; 130cm £46

● **Zigzag gold-silver/White ZipDisc**
The gold-silver side combines gold and silver for added warmth to the subject.
56cm £15; 81cm £26; 107cm £37

● **Silver/white ZipDisc**
The classic hand-held reflector. Supplied with a zip case.
56cm £15; 81cm £26; 107cm £37

● **ZipDisc Four-colour cover**
This four-colour (gold, white, silver and black) sleeve cover can be used on any round or oval reflector.
56cm (22in) ZipDisc reversible: £13
81cm (32in) ZipDisc reversible: £15
107cm (42in) ZipDisc reversible: £16

● **5-in-1 kit**
This is a combination of the ZipDisc translucent panel and the four-colour sleeve. We've tested the 81cm 5-in-1 in our comparison test.
56cm £21; 81cm £34; 107cm £41

Please note that if you visit Calumet's website, you may get a little confused about the product descriptions, so if you've any queries, phone the customer service line on 08706 030303.

Elemental

www.studio-flash.com

Budget studioflash specialists Elemental currently only has two collapsible reflectors in its range, but we've included them in this guide as they represent excellent value for money. Both the 80cm and 107cm 5-in-1 kits comprise a white diffuser with an interchangeable gold, silver and white reflector cover, all supplied in a black bag. The 80cm costs £25, while the 107cm is £35. Elemental also has a reflector arm available for £25.

Interfit

www.interfitphotographic.com

Interfit is one of the UK's leading brands of studio equipment and has an extensive range of reflectors, from hand-helds to larger stand-supported types, so you've plenty of choice!

● Soft sun/white; silver/white and silver/gold
Round, collapsible reflectors available in three finishes and four sizes.
30cm £10.50; **56cm** £16.50; **82cm** £27.60; **107cm** £39

● 5-in-1 kits
These feature a translucent reflector, with a four-colour overlay sleeve (gold, silver, black and white), supplied in a zip-up bag. They are available in three sizes, as follows.
56cm £26.50; **82cm** £37; **107cm** £44

● Easy Grip
Interfit's Easy Grip reflector has a thick handle for one-handed use and measures 90x60cm (36x24in). It is available in the following colours: sunlight/white; gold/silver; silver/white and ½-stop translucent and costs £40.

● Portrait Reflector Kit
Interfit's Portrait Reflector Kit is essentially three reflector panels attached to a frame that fits easily on a lighting stand. Each 90x60cm (36x24in) panel can be individually positioned for improved lighting control. The kit is supplied with one silver/gold panel and two sunlight/silver panels, and costs £100.

● The Large Flat Panel Reflector
Studio-based photographers may be interested in these large reflector panels, made for full-length portraits and fashion shoots. The Large Flat Panel Reflector measures 89x178cm (35x70in) and is supplied complete with a stand and a rotating/tilting bracket for using the panel vertically or horizontally. Silver/gold and white/black versions are available for £82.

● Flexi-lite 5-in-1
This stand-mounted panel reflector is aimed at pros and can be used hand-held or on location. The aluminium frame has a boon arm that can be positioned at any angle. Various kits are available in medium (100x150cm) or large (150x200cm). The INT303 has a gold/silver/black/white cover and costs £306.

Lastolite

www.lastolite.com

Lastolite is one of the world's leading studio accessory brands and is particularly renowned for its lighting aids, so it's no surprise to discover it has an extensive range of products. Many are designed for specific pro uses, so due to space constraints, we've selected the products most suitable for general portrait photography. A comprehensive brochure PDF can be downloaded from Lastolite's website if you'd like to check out the entire range.

● Collapsible reflectors:
When it comes to collapsible reflectors, no brand has as many options as Lastolite. Its round reflectors are available in 30cm, 50cm, 76cm, 95cm and 120cm diameters and there is a huge 1.8x1.2m rectangular option, too. All of these are available in the following finishes: silver/white; Sunfire/white, silver/gold, Sunfire/silver; gold/white and Sunlite/soft silver. A two-stop diffuser is also available in all sizes from 50cm upwards. Guide prices for silver/white are as follows.
30cm £13; **50cm** £24; **75cm** £35; **95cm** £58; **120cm** £75; **1.8x1.2m** £91

● Bottletops 5-in-1 kit:
This includes a diffuser panel with elasticated covers. The kit comprises the diffuser panel and a gold/white and Sunfire/silver cover and comes in four sizes: 50cm (£41), 75cm (£47), 95cm (£57) and 120cm (£85).

● TriGrip:
The original TriGrip was the first collapsible reflector to feature a handle and proved extremely popular. The design has been updated, with a new moulded handle improving handling and there are now three sizes in the range: the £47 Mini TriGrip (45cm); £62 TriGrip (75cm) and £77 Large TriGrip (1.2m). For each size, you can choose reflectors in silver/white, gold/white, Sunfire/silver and Sunlite/Softsilver finishes, as well as a one-stop or two-stop diffuser. Accessories for the TriGrip include a support bracket and the TriFlip, a set of seven reflector covers that can be placed over a TriGrip to offer the ultimate in versatility. You can also buy a £185 TriFlip 8:1 kit that supplies a two-stop diffuser (Mini TriGrip or TriGrip) with seven colour sleeves.

● Triflector:
The MkII kit consists of a support frame with three collapsible panels, all easily packed away in a case weighing a total of only 1.2kg. The panels are available in the following reflective finishes: Sunfire/silver, silver/white, gold/white and a 1.2-stop diffuser. A kit is £123; extra sets of panels range from £33-£45.

● UpLite 4:1:
A set of self-supporting 120x90cm reflector panels for use by photographers working on their own, who need to bounce light at an angle from the floor. The angle can be adjusted from 30-80° and the two panels can also be separated for hand-held use. The UpLite comes in two versions: the Cool Tone has sunlite/softsilver and silver/white reflective surfaces; while the Warm Tone has gold/white and Sunfire/silver reflective surfaces. It comes supplied with a waterproof shower cap and a carry case, and costs £120.

● Skylite:
Best suited for serious photographers looking for a lightweight, durable and large diffuser that can also double up as a reflector. The rigid, hollow aluminium frame supports a diffuser (0.75 or 1.25 stop) or reflector (gold/silver, silver/white, black/white or Sunfire/white) via secure Velcro fastenings. The Skylite can be bought in a number of kit forms and three sizes are available as follows: small 1.1x1.1m (1.3kg); medium 1x2m (2kg) and large 2x2m (2.3kg). The standard kit includes the frame, silver/white and translucent fabrics and carry bag, and are priced at around £138, £180 and £260 for the small, medium and large respectively.

Robust, stable, water-resistant, comfortable to carry and full of thought-out details

This is what makes the Rexton Camera bag series a reliable outdoor companion for everyone! With our 10 year guarantee on all Rexton models, this is a series you can continuously count on to protect your equipment while you are on the move.

Imaging

Entertainment

Computer

Mobile

Gaming

Sat Nav

Home & Living

The smart solution

5-in-1 reflector kits

If you're looking to buy your first lighting aid, make it one of these 5-in-1 kits. They offer silver, white, gold and (rarely used) black finishes to suit a variety of shooting situations. The translucent panel, which these reflective sleeves wrap around, can be used as a soft white reflector, although its efficiency is poor. You can also use it to shade your subject, but we'd recommend purchasing a purpose-built diffuser too as it works far better. As we've discovered when conducting this test, in all areas including build quality, the kits are very similar, so for most photographers, the cheapest option may well be the best one. We've highlighted the major differences below but in truth, they're all very similar products.

Elemental 5-in-1 (107cm)
www.studio-flash.com

Guide Price: £35
Street Price: £35

Better known for their excellent range of budget studioflash equipment, Elemental also offers a couple of 5-in-1 reflector kits that represent excellent value. This 107cm kit comes in its own black zip-up bag and once removed, the 5-in-1 reflector looks and handles much like the similarly-priced Interfit. The translucent panel is nicely manufactured and the coloured sleeve has a slot for the panel's tab to slip through when zipped up. The sleeve can be used to give a silver/black or gold/white effect and is thick and well put together. This is a great budget option and excellent value for money.

Verdict

An excellent budget buy.

Build quality (panel)	★★★★★
Build quality (sleeve)	★★★★☆
Versatility	★★★★☆
Performance	★★★★★
Value for money	★★★★★
OVERALL	★★★★★

Interfit 265 (107cm)
www.interfitphotographic.com

Guide Price: £44
Street Price: £38

The white surface of the well-made translucent panel offers a ½-stop efficiency and has a thick black edge and small cloth tab for hanging off a hook. The sleeve is made from thick material and can be wrapped around to give silver/black or gold/white options. The zip has a smooth action and at its end, the sleeve has a gap for the tab to stick through. Interfit makes a large number of reflector kits so you should have no trouble finding the most suitable size for you. Better still, they're available at an excellent price. A high-quality piece of equipment, supplied in a well-constructed zip-up black bag.

Verdict

An excellent, affordable kit.

Build quality (panel)	★★★★★
Build quality (sleeve)	★★★★☆
Versatility	★★★★☆
Performance	★★★★★
Value for money	★★★★★
OVERALL	★★★★★

Lastolite Bottletop 4896 (120cm)
www.lastolite.com

Guide Price: £85
Street Price: £80

This 120cm kit is the largest in the range, and also the biggest and most expensive 5-in-1 in our test. It's also different in a number of ways. First, the 5-in-1 kit is made up of a panel and two reversible elasticated sleeves: a gold/white and a silver/sunfire. This has a number of benefits: it's quicker to change from one to another as there is no zip, and you can fit one over each side of the panel, allowing you to have different combinations to suit your liking. The build quality is first-rate, and spare panels are available so you can place a sleeve on each and have two reflectors at the ready.

Verdict

Versatile and made to last.

Build quality (panel)	★★★★★
Build quality (sleeve)	★★★★★
Versatility	★★★★★
Performance	★★★★★
Value for money	★★★★☆
OVERALL	★★★★★

Flash accessories for portraits

There are a wide variety of lighting accessories available for your flashgun, which while not essential for general snaps, can make a difference when you're trying to be more creative with your photography. We highlight a selection of the best diffusers, softboxes and kits for your flashgun

WHILE SOME PHOTOGRAPHERS prefer to only use available light, a true master is able to sculpt light from many sources, with one of the most common being the good old flashgun. Flash is fantastic for supplementing light to get a better exposure, but they can also be used to override the ambient light for creative results. While a direct, naked flash is sufficient for some situations, many photographers frown on this basic approach as the light's rarely flattering and control is limited. So for professional results you need to start looking at adding some complementary accessories to your flash outfit to modify the light to suit the effect you want.

Before picking from the plethora of accessories available, you need to understand the difference between hard and soft light and know the flash effect you want to achieve. In basic terms, hard light produces strong shadows with sharp edges and high contrast, while one that casts weak shadows, with no definite edge, is soft light. You also need to decide if want the light to be dispersed and natural-looking or harsh and more selective. The following selection covers every type of accessory that your flashgun could ever need!

Stofen Omni-bounce

Guide Price: £17   **Street Price:** £11
www.newprouk.co.uk

Some flashguns come supplied with a clip-on diffuser, but if yours doesn't, buy a Stofen. They are devilishly effective in softening the light from your flashgun, with many snappers leaving them attached for all their on-camera flash shooting. They're available for almost every flashgun. Well worth the modest outlay.

OVERALL ★★★★★

Main types of flash accessories

Most flash modifiers fall into one of the following five categories, although some may also overlap

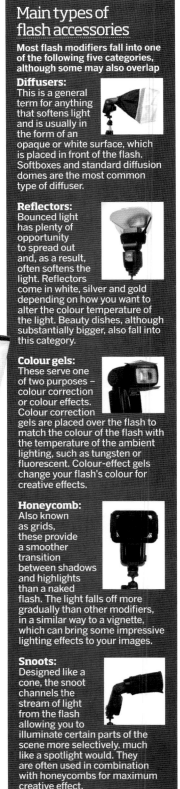

Diffusers:
This is a general term for anything that softens light and is usually in the form of an opaque or white surface, which is placed in front of the flash. Softboxes and standard diffusion domes are the most common type of diffuser.

Reflectors:
Bounced light has plenty of opportunity to spread out and, as a result, often softens the light. Reflectors come in white, silver and gold depending on how you want to alter the colour temperature of the light. Beauty dishes, although substantially bigger, also fall into this category.

Colour gels:
These serve one of two purposes – colour correction or colour effects. Colour correction gels are placed over the flash to match the colour of the flash with the temperature of the ambient lighting, such as tungsten or fluorescent. Colour-effect gels change your flash's colour for creative effects.

Honeycomb:
Also known as grids, these provide a smoother transition between shadows and highlights than a naked flash. The light falls off more gradually than other modifiers, in a similar way to a vignette, which can bring some impressive lighting effects to your images.

Snoots:
Designed like a cone, the snoot channels the stream of light from the flash allowing you to illuminate certain parts of the scene more selectively, much like a spotlight would. They are often used in combination with honeycombs for maximum creative effect.

Hama Uni Flash Diffuser

Guide Price: £20   **Street Price:** £16
www.hama.co.uk

A basic flash diffuser that has been made to fit most flashguns on the market. It can be secured to the flashgun with its own Velcro strap, making it suitable for use in the field. The price is a little high but it's worth keeping one in your camera bag should you have to use a flashgun unit you're not familiar with.

OVERALL ★★★★☆

Lumiquest Softbox III

Guide Price: £45   **Street Price:** £40
www.newprouk.co.uk

The largest of the Lumiquest range, the Softbox III produces an extremely soft light that is no easy feat when you take the size and portability of it into account. One of the reasons for the great light is that the centre of the front panel is thicker than the edges, which reduces the possibility of a hot spot caused by the head of the flashgun.

OVERALL ★★★★★

Lastolite Ezybox kit (38cm)

Guide Price: £170   **Street Price:** £160
www.johnsons-photopia.co.uk

While many of the other products have a slight 'DIY' appearance to them, the Ezybox oozes quality and build stability like nothing else in this test. While the Ezybox is value for money for pros, its high price may prove too much for most enthusiasts, even though it offers such good performance.

OVERALL ★★★★★

Speedlight Pro Beauty Dish

Guide Price: £67   **Street Price:** £67
www.speedlightprokit.co.uk

When you see the dish in its pre-assembled state, you'd be forgiven for having low expectations. However, once you put it all together things start to look up and then the results blow you away. The value for money is outstanding, as is the quality of the light it produces. One of the best accessories on the market!

OVERALL ★★★★★

Honl Flash Kit

Guide Price: £130
Street Price: £110

www.flaghead.co.uk

Contains: Two straps, 1/4 Grid, 1/8 Grid, 8in Snoot, 5in Snoot, Gobo bounce card, Colour Correction Kit, Colour Effects Kit

It's not often that a range of products comes along and changes the way that photographers work. But the Honl kit has done just that. The snoots and bounce cards are made from high-grade webbing, which can take the rigours of heavy use. Many of these accessories are available separately but this bundle offers great value for money.

Bounce card The most obvious use for this card is to use the white side to bounce light off and to soften the light landing on your subject. But it can be used for much more than that. If you get two you then have a simple set of barn doors that allow you to control the spill of the light across your image.

8in & 5in snoots The Honl snoots are very versatile pieces of kit, which lend themselves to a number of applications. They can be used closed to direct the light from your flashgun in a very direct, almost spotlight manner, so you can highlight one element in your camera's viewfinder. Alternatively,

you can open the snoot, which works in the same manner as a bounce card, directing the light up and forward towards your subject.

1/4 Grid & 1/8 Grid Spots These grids look and feel very robust and attach to your flashgun using the Speed Strap (included in the kit). Once attached the strap's strong Velcro holds incredibly well so you'll have no worries about the grids slipping.

Colour Correction Gel & Colour Effects Kit Possibly the highlight of the Honl kit, these easy-to-use gels are fast becoming one of the most popular accessories to use for making flash photography more creative. The gels have Velcro edges and attaching them to the flashgun using the Speed Strap is easy and hassle-free as you just place the gel over the flash and push on the Velcro until it takes hold. Just like the Honl grids, the gels stay in place securely and cover the whole flashgun.

Verdict
The price isn't low but the quality of the kit is superb. The outfit slips easily into just about any camera bag, weighs next to nothing and is really simple to set up.

Build quality	★★★★★
Features	★★★★★
Performance	★★★★★
Value for money	★★★★☆

OVERALL ★★★★★

Interfit Strobies Portrait Flash Kit

Guide Price: £120
Street Price: £100

www.interfitphotographic.com

Contains: Flashgun Mount, Globe, Beauty dish, Softbox, Barndoors, Snoot and Honeycomb

The Interfit Strobies kit is a scaled down version of larger studio accessories, so while the attachments are fairly sturdy, they aren't very compact or easy to transport, particularly the Globe option that is shaped like a small football. The accessories attach to a mount before they fit to a flashgun, so you'll need a separate mount if you wish to use more than one flashgun at a same time, which is highly likely.

Softbox The softbox is a miniature version of the one you get in studios and is also just as difficult to assemble. We would only recommend this softbox for a home studio as you wouldn't want to put it together more than once. That said, once assembled, the build quality is decent and as long as it isn't given too much abuse, it should give you a good few years of service.

Beauty dish The small beauty dish can be slipped on to the kit's standard mount and, despite its compact size, delivers an even spread of light. Unlike some

models, when attached, this lightweight dish won't make your flashgun feel top-heavy.

Globe diffuser This is an unusual piece of equipment that attaches to your flashgun via a supplied mount. For the best results, you will have to set your flashgun head to bounce (so it's pointing towards the ceiling) before attaching the diffuser. Once triggered, the dome fills with light and then emits the light in a spherical direction. Be careful when attaching the Globe, as one fall on to a hard surface will most likely crack it into pieces.

Barndoors Featuring four flaps, Barndoors allow you to 'cover up' some of the light from your flashgun for more control over its distribution. When using the barndoors fully open, the light from the flashgun spreads over a wide area and makes an ideal accessory for a background light. The build quality is okay, but doesn't match the Honl kit.

Snoot & Honeycomb
The Snoot and Honeycomb work in combination with each other. With the Snoot fixing to the mount, it can be used on its own to create a spotlight. The Honeycomb grid slides down the barrel of the Snoot and is dense enough to block the light quite well.

Verdict
This kit has some useful applications and would prove a frugal and rewarding buy for the photographers taking their first steps with flashgun accessories.

Build quality	★★★★☆
Features	★★★★☆
Performance	★★★★☆
Value for money	★★★★☆

OVERALL ★★★★☆

BJORN THOMASSEN

Metered to perfection!
Scenes with strong backlighting can lead to exposure error. Use a grey card and you should have no problems.

How to use your metering & White Balance cards

The 18% grey card can be used to ensure perfect exposures when shooting in tricky lighting conditions. Both reference cards can also be used to set a custom White Balance, but how you do this depends on your camera (refer to your camera's manual). In the meantime, here is a brief explanation to get you started

DIGITAL CAMERAS USE sophisticated exposure systems with a choice of metering patterns to suit different lighting situations. The systems work on the assumption that the area of the scene being metered is a mid-tone, or 18% grey to be precise; the average if all dark, light and mid-tones were mixed together. It's the basis of all metering patterns and works surprisingly well, but can render incorrect exposures when the overall scene or subject is considerably lighter or darker than 18% grey. For example, very dark areas can fool the metering system into overexposing the image, while a very light areas can fool the camera into underexposure, as the light meter will take a reading that renders it as a mid-tone.

As a camera is trying to render an image 'grey', it's your job to ensure you compensate to keep the tones true to life. You can do this by either using one of your camera's exposure override facilities, such as exposure compensation, the AE-Lock button or by metering from an area of the scene that has a mid-tone. And that's where our grey card comes in. Using it is very simple as our step-by-step guide below illustrates.

The key thing to remember is that you need to place the grey card in similar lighting to your subject, for instance, don't place it in a shaded area if your subject is bathed in sunlight. Also, make sure that the card fills the metering area – we would recommend you use spot or partial metering as the card won't need to fill the entire image area – but any is suitable. You can either lock the exposure using your camera's AE-Lock facility or note the aperture and shutter speed, then switch to manual mode and dial in these settings. This latter method isn't suitable on days where lighting is variable. The card has AF reference lines to help your camera's autofocus lock on to it. However, you don't necessarily need it to be in focus to work correctly. The grey card (as well as the white card) can also be used to take a custom White Balance reading from too.

1 Getting started If you're shooting portraits in difficult lighting conditions, such as backlighting, give your subject the grey card and ask them to hold it angled towards you.

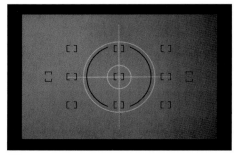

2 Take a meter reading Ensure that the entire metering area is filled by the grey card (in this instance we're using spot metering) and lock the exposure with the AE-Lock button.

3 Compose & shoot With this exposure locked, you can compose your scene and take your shots. When you check it on your LCD monitor, the exposure should be perfect.